Leadership Redefined

Leaders Reimagined

Improving Lives one Leader at a Time

Heather Ferguson

This publication is designed to provide competent and reliable information regarding the subject matter covered. It is sold with the understanding that the author and publisher specifically disclaim any liability that is incurred from the use or application of the contents of this book.

ISBN: 978-1-7359826-0-1 (Paperback)

Printed in the United States of America

Book cover designed by Frank Shaw
Book edited by Valerie Lunsford

First printing edition 2021

Printing and Distribution managed by:
S. Colton Company

www.fergusonlearning.com

TABLE OF CONTENTS

FOREWORD

MY FIRST LESSON IN LEADERSHIP

Like many of you, I have had enough mediocre bosses to last a lifetime. You can spot them from a mile away. Now good bosses, I can count those on one hand. Thankfully, those bosses were leaders who trusted and challenged me not only to develop and grow to my full potential but also encouraged me to follow my passion. As is becoming the new norm, I have had more bosses than years I have been in the workforce. I can honestly say I have learned from each one of them. Some, how to be a better leader and others are fodder within these pages. We'll get to that later, but that is not where this story begins.

While I have spent a large part of my career helping leaders reach their full potential, ironically my first and most valuable lesson in leadership didn't come from work at all. It came from Coach Bessolman. He was 6'1, a former Army Ranger with forearms like cannons, and to call him rough around the edges would be an understatement. He wasn't the type to host social gatherings; I am not even sure if his neighbors knew his name.

When he wasn't spending time with his family, he was on a baseball field. Time was never an investment in his mind; coaching was his passion. He was happy to help any player who wanted to improve his game. Somehow, Coach could always see the diamond in the rough and never turned a player away. He truly lived what he believed, which is you get what you give and people will live up to your expectations, good or bad.

He worked his players hard, but somehow the boys understood he only expected what each player was capable of giving. As long as they gave their best, he was proud of their endeavors even when the outcome wasn't what the team hoped for.

I asked Coach one time why he put so much energy into these boys, when they weren't even his kids. His response was simply, "Everyone deserves to have someone believe in them." Now I didn't completely appreciate the wisdom at the time, but in hindsight, this was a glimpse into who he really was at his core. Coach genuinely cared for those around him, be it his wife and children, or the extended baseball family he created over the years.

Coach hung up his cleats when his youngest son went off to college. He wanted to spend time with his grandchildren and refused to miss his son's baseball games. Those around him worried about how he would do after coaching for over 20 years, but he was okay with his decision. He said that he had done all he could do, now he wanted to sit back and enjoy watching his players become the men he expects them to be. He would run into his boys from time to time and they would always take a few minutes to catch up before going on about their busy lives. I remember thinking one time how sad it must be to devote so much time and energy into something and get nothing in return.

Coach lived the life he loved, spending his last day on Earth at a baseball tournament with his son. Around the dinner table that night, he recapped each play for the rest of the family. Coach passed away in a heartbeat at the age of 50 with his small family around him. As they made the funeral arrangements, they realized that he didn't have any friends to notify. His daughter was worried about no one else being there; she suggested they each drive separately so that there would be more cars.

When the dreaded day arrived, the family got into four cars and followed one another to the services. Can a day get worse? You bet. There was a traffic jam on the four-lane highway at the entrance to the cemetery and it seemed that every car was determined to impede their path.

As they finally managed to get pulled in, there were cars lined on both sides of the driveway and no parking spots to be found. His daughter was indignant that the only space for their pitiful party of four cars seemed to be a half a mile walk from where the services would be held. As the family walked together, her heart sank as she realized that her father's service was being held directly next to this huge service.

The funeral director walked over and shook hands with the family. The daughter said, "We are all here; we can get started with the service." The gentleman looked confused as he looked around and said, "Well, ma'am, we can't get started just yet. There are still people trying to get in; they are out on the road. It will take a bit of time." She scanned the crowd of obnoxious people who had blocked their way and taken all the parking spots, suddenly recognizing some of the boys she once knew. Now they were grown men, many surrounded by their families, but these were his kids. They had come in from across the states to be there and pay their respects.

It was at that moment that I realized what leadership really is. I knew my Dad cared, but I didn't see the rest of the picture. When you care for others -- not because you will get something in return, but because it is the right thing to do -- the impact you can have is priceless.

INTRODUCTION

As an HR Partner to the business, a coach, and a mentor to leaders across industries and geographies, I have spent years teaching others how to successfully make the transition from manager to People Leader. I fundamentally believe that all employees strongly desire to be fulfilled in their jobs, to have opportunities to grow while achieving their personal and professional goals. This accomplishment can only occur if employees are not managed as tools but rather are understood, appreciated, and led as talented individuals.

This book is intended to challenge all manners in which you function as a leader. I will highlight the flaws in how far too many companies choose to operate today. The ultimate goal is to push you outside of your comfort zone and illustrate for you that there is a way for you to become the people leader your team needs you to be.

Organizational hierarchies have evolved and become more complex over time. This has resulted in a dramatic change in management roles and responsibilities. The intricacy of most organizations today includes multiple locations across geographies with matrixed reporting structures. This top-heavy framework results in nearly everyone focusing on the numbers, leaving very few leaders contemplating the overall talent health that is needed for future growth and sustainability.

Most companies across the globe are expressing concerns that they do not have the talent necessary within their organization to achieve their long-term goals. More specifically, there is an understanding that people leadership is one of the greatest deficits that must be addressed. But how is that possible? There are countless people employed around the world who are responsible for overseeing other people. At the foundation of the problem is the fact that most organizations are staffed with managers, not People Leaders. There is a distinct difference.

The fact is the world is changing at an unprecedented rate. The days of joining a company from school and remaining through retirement have passed. Unfortunately, companies have not adjusted their operational practices to keep up with the change in this employee-driven marketplace.

With less time to get employees fully contributing and the increasing need to stretch the average employment length beyond five years, business models and leaders must evolve.

Change starts with the recognition that a company's success is dependent on its people. Having high productivity, low turnover, and high customer satisfaction does not happen by accident. This can only be achieved by phenomenal People Leaders who actively develop an engaged workforce.

As a People Leader, your responsibilities are vast, but they are nothing compared to the impact you can have. Your daily interactions have a direct and lasting effect. Never lose sight that every action or inaction counts, for highly engaged employees are created, not hired.

Leadership Redefined - Leaders Reimagined will provide you a roadmap for not only what steps need to be taken to become a Dynamic People Leader, but more importantly, how. From building trust and collaboration to flawless talent management execution, you will gain every insight, trick, and tool that I have collected over the years.

When I set out on the journey to write this book, I had one mission in mind: To *improve lives one People Leader at a time*. Your journey starts here. It is time for you to learn, grow, and pave your own distinct path forward as only you can define the leader you want to be.

Thank you for being part of this quest and allowing me to be a part of your leadership journey.

DYNAMIC LEADERSHIP

~ PEOPLE ~

People interactions are the cornerstone of Dynamic Leadership. Learn how these strong relationships produce extraordinary business results.

1

STOP MANAGING AND START LEADING

Rob and his team are buried in tasks and projects with endless deadlines. His department reaches one short-term goal just to find they are already behind in achieving the next. Rob values his team and the tremendous effort they put in week after week. He often stresses that he is not doing enough to support them, but there just aren't enough hours in the day. He hasn't figured out how to tackle the problems of today, let alone pause to think about things that are sure to come down the pike. Right now, Rob doesn't have the luxury of being forward thinking. While he feels very connected to his team as they take on the barrage of never-ending firefights, he has yet to spend sufficient time developing them for future roles they are interested in pursuing. Honestly, the thought of someone leaving his team right now piles on the stress. Rob knows his team deserves more than he is currently able to give them, but he isn't sure what, if anything, he can do about it given the current situation.

Sound familiar? If so, you are not alone. When in a similar situation, it is understandably easier to give in to the daily pressures. After all, there is a job to do. Depending on how your company defines success and the frequency in which that evaluation occurs, there are two competing methods for achieving organizational goals.

There are managers, who are focused on managing the work execution, productivity, and results. This is their primary concern and the core driver of all actions. They are essentially navigating through the chaos as painful as that is.

Then there are those who navigate around the chaos. They simply chose a different path to get to the same outcome. Leaders empower their team to achieve the short-term goals. The team knows what needs to be done and they choose how to make it happen. This allows their leader to focus on ensuring long-term success is attained through a clear vision, team commitment, thoughtful relationship building, and an unwavering dedication to employee development that will undoubtedly guide the organization forward. Because leaders define success very differently, the results they achieve are substantially more beneficial. Their teams don't just get the outcome or hit the numbers today; they are able to foresee and tackle the problems of tomorrow.

To be clear, the reference to being a manager has nothing to do with your job title; it has everything to do with how you choose to operate. Your designation as a manager or People Leader is earned over time. The actions you take, the behavior you exhibit, and the personal interactions you have will each play an important role in how you are perceived. This perception will then dictate how valued you are within the organization.

Managers Operate Tactically

Managers are not critical thinkers; they are executors. They are not creative problem solvers. They are simply the doers.

Managers function the way they do because performance success is measured against short-term gains. These priorities are dictated to them and they only know one way to hit the target. They focus all of their attention on the detailed tasks that will allow them to achieve the end goal. Managers process all situations or goals in the same way. Whether it is a last-minute order from an important client, a monthly quota increase, or simply the quarter end, the "how" is the same.

They put their tactical gear on and drive every detail through completion. Managers determine what needs to be done, who should do it, how it should be done, and dictate every action in between. The workers within that team are simply tools to achieve the goal or task defined by the organization. There is limited time and energy spent on developing the talent because when viewed as a tool, tools are interchangeable. "If one doesn't work, just replace it with another that will."

Not appreciating the talent under your direction will hinder and limit your potential career opportunities. Far more importantly, it has catastrophic ramifications for your company. Managers and organizations that undervalue the diverse backgrounds and experiences of their talent will miss critical opportunities to learn, improve, and evolve the way in which they operate. Becoming irrelevant will inadvertently occur the moment learning and growth are not at the forefront of the corporate culture.

This is not to say that managers are inherently flawed or have the wrong intentions. The function of a manager is the product of today's business environment. Managers have been conditioned over time to color inside the lines, always following the process, and to deliver at any cost. This manner of operating limits the ability to creatively solve problems.

In many cases, we have entry and mid-level working managers. Yes, this is a thing. As the name implies, this basically means you have a full-time job with key deliverables just like everyone else in your unit; however, in addition to that, you must manage the people-related processes for your team or department.

You notice that I said "people-related processes," not the people. With the tremendous pressures of chasing short-term profitability and quarterly operational metrics, managers have very little control. This often leaves them feeling forced to focus strictly on tasks and deadlines. After all, that is what they are measured on.

Managers like Rob are operating in a survival mindset, with actions and behaviors that tend to be very short term and tactical in nature:

"How do we get through the week"?

"Where did we miss last week; how do I countermeasure against it happening again"?

"I have a gap in the production line; when will someone show up to fill it"?

Like most people, Rob doesn't simply want to be a manager. Personally, he wants to perform well in his job. At the same time, he wants more for his team. This simple acknowledgment that he is not on par with his own expectations is enough to get him focused on making a change. See, Rob isn't satisfied with being a manager. He wants to be a people leader.

PEOPLE LEADERS OPERATE STRATEGICALLY

People Leaders are game-changers. In contrast to ordinary managers, they coach and lead their staff to achieve the necessary goals. They are less concerned with the trivial details of how things get done as long as the desired end results are achieved. Leaders build strong teams that are empowered to take ownership of the daily workflow. This approach provides employees with the opportunity to deliver against their performance objectives independently. Under this leadership approach, leaders dedicate their full focus to the long-term strategic efforts.

Leaders are naturally more collaborative and highly value partnership across the organization because they get the big picture. Leaders have a unique view of the corporate world in which they operate and a distinct vision for how to impact it. By deliberately not immersing themselves in the daily grind, they have the capacity to think broader.

Their dedication of substantial time, attention, and efforts towards being future-focused, innovative, and impactful delivers meaningful results. Achievement of the seemingly unachievable does not occur by accident. It is the outcome of an established vision that garners trust and followership. Strong relationships with these characteristics can radiate throughout the organization.

Such leaders possess a keen awareness and in-depth understanding of the organizational challenges. They exert the confidence to navigate through any barriers that may exist. How? By remaining flexible in their approach, empowering their competent and fully capable team to achieve the goals at hand, and trusting that their people will deliver. To put it plainly, they don't sweat the small stuff.

YOU MUST BE MINDFUL OF YOUR IMPACT

There is not a one-size-fits-all approach to leading people. As a leader, you must flex and adapt to each given circumstance. Whether you are hiring someone into your organization fresh off-campus or promoting someone from an hourly position to an exempt role, you are forever changing someone's life. Each milestone for an employee is a critical one for that individual, his or her family, and their future.

You have a direct and defining impact on whether the essential moments throughout the employment journey are perceived as positive or negative experiences. You are responsible for producing and ensuring the success of future generations of leaders within your company. It is because of this tremendous impact that you must remain dedicated and pay keen attention to growing your own skills and capabilities as a leader.

To be clear, there is no greater challenge than to be a people leader today. You have the demands of a complex business that pummels you at every turn. These challenging barriers and hurdles will produce constant stress for the organization. Leaders are often simultaneously working to overcome these challenges and protect their people from the madness that surrounds them. Whether it is managing competing priorities, limited time, dwindling resources, or substantial talent shortages, these issues are tackled head-on.

As though all of these issues are not enough, leaders are faced with unprecedented demographic complexity in the current workforce. Leaders are required to achieve results through relationships that span across three or, in some cases, four different generations simultaneously. They must remain mindful of how their direction will be received, interpreted, and acted upon given the demographic makeup of the team. Given the complicated nature of work today and the critical impact that leaders have on those around them, a strategic focus must be made to improve leadership capability and close competency gaps.

THE SECRET TO SUCCESS

Being a people leader has many facets; however, there are certain characteristics that help identify those who have the potential for success in such a meaningful role. Integrity, courage, confidence, ability to learn, agility, and passionate are common traits of People Leaders.

Clearly, there are many people who have some of these characteristics that are not and should not be people leaders. So, what is the secret? Add all of these with one's natural ability to care.

No matter how hard you try, caring is not a teachable trait. You either do or you don't. But, one thing is definite: Leaders who genuinely care about others, those who take pride in helping others achieve, will always build a better team. That kind of team will be more engaged and produce extraordinary results.

Just imagine for a moment a world where your entire team is not only exceedingly competent but also highly caring:

How would cross-functional relationships improve?

How would productivity change?

How would customer relationships benefit?

Like Rob, you now have a choice. Who do you choose to be? Do you want to continue managing the people and processes that are thrown at you? Or do you want more? Are you ready to learn how to stop managing and start leading?

Individuals who care deliver superior customer experiences.

Teams who care produce extraordinary results for the company.

Leaders who are caring create the environment for both to occur.

Since you are still reading, I am presuming that means you are ready and up for the challenge. Fabulous. To get us looking through a leader's lens, we have to start at the foundation. What do leaders care about most? Their people. Because leaders fundamentally believe that the people deliver the business and drive growth, they invest a great deal of time into making and keeping their people happy. As we move into the next chapter, we will discuss the Employee Experience, how that impacts Employee Engagement, and what actions can be taken to improve both.

2

EMPLOYEE ENGAGEMENT

Even as early as his initial internship interview, it was obvious David was a future leader just waiting to be groomed for a successful career. He did not disappoint. He consistently gave 110% even on his off days. Always among the first to arrive each morning and never early to leave, he set a fine example; but that was just the tip of it. He was highly engaged and excelled in every aspect of his role.

He was following a clearly defined career path and would routinely volunteer for special assignments that would hone the skills he needed to hit the ground running in his next assignment. With an exceptional work ethic and mental capacity to handle work at least two levels above his own, each organization he joined became more highly functioning. His natural leadership ability shown through in all aspects of his performance – with peers, management above him, and when working with cohorts across the company. David was clear in his career aspirations and ensured he excelled in every job assignment that would enable him to reach the next level in his climbing the corporate ladder. David worked hard and that work ethic rubbed off on those around him. He was clearly ready for a leadership role when the position became available.

Three applicants were interviewing for a position that would result in one of them landing a promotion: David met all the necessary requirements. Kimberly had two years' tenure in the department prior to David's arrival. In the time David had been there, Kimberly had never taken on a substantial project or special assignment. She met her objectives each year, but she lacked experience leading teams as it wasn't a necessary skill set in her previous roles. Her long lunch hours were common water cooler talk, but everyone acknowledged she had charisma and was well liked by the leadership team. Chelsey was also a highly engaged future leader who joined the company at the same time as David. Their fierce competition evolved into a personal friendship. He was humble and reckoned if Chelsey got the promotion, she deserved it; her contributions made everyone in their department better.

After weeks of interviews, Kimberly got the promotion. It was clear from the outset that she couldn't pull her weight as a people leader. Whether it was inaptitude, laziness, or a host of other possibilities, the team who inherited Kimberly as their leader began a steady decline under her direction.

Chelsey saw that the writing was on the wall and her disengagement drove her reaction to the situation. She quickly decided that any company who would promote individuals into leadership positions simply because they had put their time in was a company she could not see a future with. When the promoted had no intention or capability to lead, she seriously questioned the principles of the leader that made this decision without considering the peril of those who would be reporting to Kimberly. Before the next opening would become available, she had joined a close competitor of her former employer as a true leader. She now has a position where she can drive change, empower her team, and be the asset throughout the organization she always knew she could be.

David's director advised him to bide his time. He was assured that "leadership is watching him" and "his time will come; this just isn't his time." As the days and weeks pass with no additional conversations with his leader on what is next for him, David becomes increasingly more frustrated. The former highly-engaged top performer now arrives at work on time and not a minute sooner. When the clock strikes four, you can count on him to immediately head out the door. He hasn't volunteered to do anything extra. He still does his job and does it well, but he gives what he's gotten and not a bit more. His negativity and sour attitude are abundantly evident in every conversation. Office friends find it hard to believe this is the same charismatic, energetic co-worker everyone wanted to emulate just a short time ago.

David is not just disengaged; he is actively disengaged. He has completely checked out and intentionally does the bare minimum to get by. The company has his body; his mind is anywhere but on a future with this company.

Can David ever come back from this? Not likely, the relationship between David and his leaders has crumbled. There is no longer trust or respect. David is already gone; he just hasn't officially resigned yet, but he will and soon. The toxicity of a deflated, disengaged, and once highly regarded employee can be catastrophic to a department.

Promoting Kimberly may have been the right business decision or it may have been a huge error in judgment. We can't say for sure. What we do know is that the poor reaction by leaders to address employee engagement has cost this business not just one future leader; they have lost two. Unfortunately, the leadership team did not consider how critical employee engagement is; as a result, they put in no effort to avoid this outcome.

David and Chelsey show us how just one employee experience, if bad enough, can cause a complete breakdown in engagement. It is situations such as these that leave leaders feeling blindsided when their top talent resigns. They either didn't see the signs of an engagement shift or didn't think it really mattered.

Regardless of the reasoning, leaders often neglect to properly value employee experiences and how they drive engagement. This is a result of how employees are viewed. Real change will only occur when employees are treated as internal customers. When an employee's experience and engagement are as critical to the business as customer satisfaction, you will find a strong company with a balanced culture.

EMPLOYEES = INTERNAL CUSTOMERS

Increased competitiveness in today's marketplaces demands that companies remain laser-focused on delivering value to their customers. Doing so enables healthy profit margin growth. Success is completely dependent on attracting and retaining customers. Companies will invest a tremendous amount of time, energy, and money to build, as well as to maintain, those relationships. There is an expectation that significant resource allocation will result in a strong return on investment.

Customer satisfaction measured in the most basic format of product quality, price, delivery speed, and accuracy of order fulfillment misses one critical component: The human element. There are people working hard to ensure that all these metrics are attained.

Simply supplying a product or service at a good price with expeditious delivery will not warrant customer loyalty. Providing a superior customer experience should be the overarching goal that every company strives for. Raising the bar this high means that your employees must believe in the mission. Success is dependent upon everyone being fully committed.

The desire to be customer-focused is stated by most companies in some form or fashion. In actuality, very few truly operate from that frame of mind. Those that are successful in living their mission do so because their employees bring the company's mission to life.

When each of your employees feel appreciated and valued, they pass that behavior along to others. Think about it like a drive-through lane where the person in front of you pays for your lunch order. You are more likely to pass that along to the car behind you to continue the goodwill. The same applies when managing relationships of internal and external customers.

Experience has taught me that employees will treat customers in a fashion similar to how they are treated by you, their employer. When every action you take reinforces the message that the employee experience matters, your team will truly believe that they own an important role in the company mission. This collaboration will translate into sustained and measurable business results.

You will experience:

- Increased engagement scores

- Lower turnover rates

- Higher production volume

- Overall better customer satisfaction

Transforming your organization into an employee-centric environment will be a tremendous culture shift. One where every leader has a firm understanding of how to recognize critical employee experience moments and what actions are required of them in any situation they may face. An endeavor of this magnitude requires substantial time, energy, and dedication. With an expanded view of the world that functions on a framework where employees are considered essential internal customers, you will have to revisit many of the operational norms you follow today.

Pause for a moment. Imagine that your company has defined a mission to transform the organization by labeling employees as internal customers.

Ask yourself:

How would the processes and policies change?

Would my talent initiatives take a higher priority?

Would the way in which I lead my team change?

What behaviors do I need to adjust to enable myself to live out this mission every day?

Don't get me wrong, leading culture change is a grueling undertaking. You are learning new skills and likely adjusting behaviors that have been the norm for a very long time. You should not get discouraged. You already have the skill set necessary to make the transition. After all, you have a wealth of experience in managing customer relationships.

More insight will be gleaned by looking at some of the areas where you interact with external customers today. You will see how easily those actions and behaviors could translate to enable effective management of the employee experience for your internal customers.

CUSTOMERS
COMPARISON

CLIENTS	EXTERNAL	=	INTERNAL	EMPLOYEES
	MARKETING		EMPLOYER BRAND	
	PRODUCT SALES		EMPLOYER OF CHOICE	
	SALES EXECUTION		CANDIDATE CARE	
	CLIENT SERVICES		NEW HIRE ASSIMILATION	
	EXPANDING MARKET SHARE		SUCCESSION PLANNING	
	FEEDBACK LOOP		CAREER CONVERSATIONS	
	PORTFOLIO MANAGEMENT		DEVELOPMENT PLANNING	
	DIVESTITURES		PERFORMANCE IMPROVEMENT	
	CONTINUOUS IMPROVEMENT		EMPLOYEE EXPERIENCE	
	CUSTOMER LOYALTY		RETENTION	

Marketing & Employer Brand

Brand recognition is imperative to attracting customers. Through strategic tailored marketing efforts, you are targeting potential customers. The goal is to provide insight into your company while building awareness of the products you offer that will meet their specific needs. At the core, you want to be the supplier of choice when they have a need.

You can and should use the same strategies to build an employer brand. Through targeted attraction efforts, you begin to build name recognition among job seekers. The additional traffic to your career site will increase the volume of candidates available for open positions.

Product Sales & Employer of Choice

Now that you have gained the interest of a potential customer, your emphasis shifts to delivering value that differentiates you from the competition. This is when having a superior product or portfolio is tremendously helpful to fend off any market competitors.

For job seekers active in the employment search, this phase highlights the unique attributes your company has to offer. At this point, it is about convincing potential applicants that engaging with your company is in their best interests. There is not one standard benefit or perk that will meet the needs of all candidates. Some companies focus on work-life balance, some on diversity and inclusion, while others focus on compensation. Each is a strategy designed to attract and engage the unique candidate who values that specific offering.

Sales Execution & Candidate Care

So, the interest remains. Now you are ready to ink the deal. Every interaction between your team and the customer must be flawlessly executed to ensure that you can close the sale. Whether it is a phone call or a face-to-face meeting, your customers should walk away feeling supported and appreciated. Providing an exceptional customer experience will be the foundation you will use to build and maintain the relationship moving forward.

In the case of employment, this process is referred to as "candidate care." From the application to offer, encompassing every interaction in between, there is a bilateral focus underway. The internal focus is on speed. Companies measure time to fill vacant positions because there is an understanding that for every day a vacancy exists the company is losing money. The external focus is on feelings. More specifically, making preferred candidates feel unique and special.

Client Services & New Hire Assimilation

Ensuring a smooth integration is the primary necessity as new customers come on board. Some refer to this function as client services or customer service. This group is tasked with the responsibility of making sure that the clients' needs are fully met. Equipping customers with the knowledge necessary to feel confident in using your products or services is the fundamental objective.

The same type of integration occurs as part of the new-hire assimilation process. The basic premise of assimilation is that by providing employees with a structured plan they will have a greater chance at success. This systematic approach to foundational learning will build each new hires' confidence in their capabilities to execute in his or her new role. With this, they will be able to contribute to the business more quickly.

Expanding Market Share & Succession Planning

Growth in the traditional format involves the constant expansion of market share. In the rush to penetrate new markets and expand existing networks, there are two distinct strategies of execution. One is through innovation. The other is by way of acquisitions. There are companies on the cutting edge of technology that are strategically focused on creating the next innovative business solution. Often this ground-breaking work is resolving a problem that consumers are not even aware they have. The alternative approach to obtaining growth is through the acquisition of smaller companies with upside potential.

As the business landscape changes, applying this same sense of urgency and competitiveness into developing the next generation of future leaders will be essential to the long-term success of the organization. For succession planning to be fruitful, you must have the capability to recognize and identify high-potential talent throughout the organization. Those individuals must be provided key learning assignments and career progression opportunities to encourage and sustain continued development.

Feedback Loop & Career Conversations

Companies that are customer driven spend significant time getting to know what challenges their customers are constrained by. This insight enables them to recognize where solutions may be provided. They are then able to assist their clients in achieving their ultimate goals.

Employee-driven companies prioritize specific actions that help them understand what their employees' career aspirations are. Focused efforts are dedicated to identifying and removing existing obstacles that may hinder the attainment of those goals. As a people leader, you must remain committed to helping each individual employee reach his or her full potential. This level of comprehension can only be achieved through the execution of frequent, meaningful career conversations.

Portfolio Management & Development Planning

Portfolio management involves performance monitoring of all products and services. Continuous observation and ongoing data collection are fundamental necessities. Strategic analysis will highlight untapped opportunities to expand current relationships or product capabilities.

For internal customers, development planning is the primary mechanism by which opportunities to expand an employee's capabilities are reviewed. To ensure employee growth is properly identified, documented, and executed you will need to act collaboratively with your employee. A successful partnership will require you to actively participate in frequent, ongoing discussions with your employee.

Divestitures & Performance Improvement

There are times when products or divisions are not producing the necessary return on investment (ROI). Strong market competitiveness means companies rarely have the luxury of time. Leaders understand that success in this situation means being decisive. Timely action is necessary to eliminate the potential for future losses.

Despite your best efforts, there are times when an employee's performance is not where it needs to be. As a people leader, it is your responsibility to execute all avenues of performance improvement available to you. If at that point the employee is still not meeting expectations specific to the role, you should be equally as decisive and timely when ending the employment relationship.

Continuous Improvement & Employee Experience

Companies seek to improve the customer experience and overall satisfaction by frequently collecting voice of customer (VOC) data. Strategic actions are then executed based on the information obtained. This drive to continuously improve the offered products and services based on customer needs maintains the company's competitiveness in the marketplace.

Companies that strive to improve the overall employee experience will frequently gain employee insights through the collection of voice of employee (VOE) data. Armed with this information, swift and meaningful actions are taken to meet the needs defined by employees.

Customer Loyalty & Retention

Striving to keep customers happy so that they will remain loyal is paramount to the company's stability. Fluctuation in the customer base has a direct correlation to the company's profitability. These business results can cause drastic swings in the stress of the overall organization.

To achieve your company goals, a stable workforce is a necessity. Managing retention risks and monitoring employee turnover is less of a burden when your effort is on keeping your employees fulfilled in their careers. Employees who are encouraged to do work that they love to do are generally more satisfied. Those empowered are less likely to look for a new opportunity outside the company.

EMPLOYEE EXPERIENCE JOURNEY

Recruitment	Assimilation	Development	Departure
Attraction	Onboarding	Career Conversations & Development	Offboarding
Candidate Care	Immersion	Succession Planning	
Pre-hire		Performance Management	

EVERY EMPLOYEE EXPERIENCE MATTERS

As you can see, the employee experience is a journey. All employees undertake this path from the moment they first learn who your company is to the time when they part ways with the organization. There is a cumulative impact of these crucial employee experience moments that undoubtedly influence the employee's overall engagement.

Leaders understand that every moment and every single interaction matters. They can see the correlation between positive employee experiences and the successes of their team. Consequently, leaders choose to take ownership of the role they play. They give thoughtful consideration as to how their behaviors directly impact and influence an employee's experience and, ultimately, overall engagement.

Fully appreciating the employee experience journey will empower you to evaluate situations from an employee-centric mindset. This enables you to make decisions that are both logical and thoughtful. By doing so, you are better poised to achieve outstanding business results that will simultaneously enable your employees to be fulfilled within their roles and careers.

When you care about the members of your team, you will continually strive to provide them with an exceptional employee experience.

Looking back to David and Chelsey, would you have handled the situation differently understanding that this was a critical moment in the employees' employee experience journey? What would you have done to keep both David and Chelsey full engaged and still part of your team?

Employees are constantly interpreting, analyzing, and reflecting on the experiences and interactions that occur. These data points drive how engaged they are at any given moment. This knowledge will enable you to avoid common pitfalls, think more strategically, and truly enhance the lives of those who work for and around you.

WHAT IS EMPLOYEE ENGAGEMENT?

Employee engagement defines how satisfied employees are with you, their team, and the company as a whole. The more engaged your employees are, the greater discretionary effort they will expend for the teams benefit. It is no secret that high employee engagement correlates to lower turnover and higher productivity. The question becomes: Who are these highly engaged people and how do you find them?

These are the employees who will go above and beyond to deliver for the customer. They love what they do and it shows. Not only are fully engaged employees more productive than their counterparts, they generally have a positive outlook on even the most challenging situations and are excited about the future. Highly engaged staff members role model the behaviors that we all want our employees to exhibit. We would clone them if we could!

It is important to grasp that highly engaged employees are not hired; they are created as a product of the company culture. A business that takes the time to focus on its employees' well-being will find a greater population of these folks embedded throughout the organization.

Conversely, companies with a limited appreciation for their employees and the work they produce will find it is significantly harder to get work done. Collaboration across the organization will be halted by a siloed approach to work execution and a disengaged workforce with no desire to resolve the challenges that are impacting productivity.

WHO IS RESPONSIBLE FOR ENGAGEMENT?

There is a great debate underway as to who owns employee engagement. Traditional minds operate under the notion that the Human Resources Department is responsible for all employee-related initiatives; however, that is a fallacy. There is no one sole owner of employee engagement. If you accept this as fact, then you can progress the conversation to what really matters, point of impact. What interactions and experiences have the most influential impact on the employee base?

Within your business, everyone has a crucial role to play when ensuring that employees are fully engaged. Whether it is an employee contributing feedback, a direct supervisor ensuring career development, HR providing coaching, or the CEO driving culture change, no one is exempt.

Every leader needs to have a strong relationship with HR. Building and maintaining this partnership is fundamental to the success of both you and your team. A good HR partner's job with regards to employee engagement starts with keeping both you and the organization honest from an accountability standpoint. Are you actively listening to employee feedback, taking the appropriate actions, and truly doing all that you can to drive positive employee experiences?

The only way circumstances improve is if there is real effort put behind change initiatives, which means sometimes you may need a push to get things going and to keep on track. Your HR Partner will help you determine where you should be focusing your efforts to ensure impactful change. They will provide you with specific coaching and offer guidance for ways to bring about change within your team as well as the broader organization.

The proper identification of improvement opportunities will be an ongoing collaborative process. Your HR Partner will offer suggestions and recommendations for ways to address employee concerns, resolve existing conflicts, and coach you through the change management process when necessary. Ultimately, your HR Partner is tasked with holding you accountable for delivering on your commitments.

As a leader, your daily interactions have a direct and lasting impact on employee engagement. Understanding the existing workplace challenges, what barriers are hindering success, and what development gaps exist are all important matters you must be aware of. Being cognizant of perceptions, negative feelings, or challenges is not enough. This knowledge demands you take swift, decisive, and specific action toward improving the workplace and operating environment for the betterment of all.

Additionally, you have a responsibility to build your awareness as to how the individual members of your team impact their cross-functional counterparts. Your team can have awesome engagement amongst themselves, but if teams upstream or downstream are negatively impacted by your group you have a vital role to play in resolving the problem.

In an employee-centric environment, collaboration is vitally important. Companies cannot allow one group to succeed by standing on the head of another team. Strong culture is reinforced through a common set of principles. To be sustained over time trust, respect, and collaboration must be front and center.

As harsh as it may sound, as a leader you are only as good as the leaders you leave behind. The higher you progress in your career, the further you will move away from the day-to-day execution. That is why you must make sure that the culture you have built will be maintained once you are no longer there to guide the team and their daily interactions.

Your legacy is dependent on the team and leaders you have developed to carry the torch forward. Now that doesn't mean you get promoted and you are out of the engagement business. It is actually the complete opposite.

As a senior leader, you will need to work even harder to stay connected to the people within your span of control. Regardless of your level, you should constantly be looking for new and better ways to improve the employee experience for your teams. While your engagement role may now be one that acts as an advisor or coach, you must remain actively involved. Never become complacent and lose sight of the fact that if you are not caring for your employees there is a People Leader out there who will.

OWN IT OR CHANGE IT

With the engagement of employees being linked to not only the company culture but also to the culture of your team, you must first conduct a little honest self-reflection. Both people leaders and executives need to consider and analyze the following questions:

As a company, who are we and how do we truly operate?

As a team, who are we and how do we truly operate?

How do my actions and behaviors have an impact?

Now you must decide. Do you like who you are as an organization or as a team? If yes, then own it! If you like being the hard-working company where not everyone can cut it and only the strong will survive, then own it. There are many companies that are known for high turnover and it is a badge of honor to be employed with those establishments for an extended period of time.

As a company or a team, if you don't like how you are operating, then change it! It is within your control to establish a new vision or adjust the organizational priorities. To achieve substantial improvement in your business results you must expect, own, and drive profound change. Do not attempt baby steps.

You do not have the luxury of time. Be bold. Take the action you know is needed. Lead your company to the forefront. Have trust in each and every employee within your organization to bring this mission to fruition. You must strongly communicate the vision in a way that everyone will hear and understand the new expectations.

In an ideal world, all businesses would execute their strategic objectives based on an employee-centric framework. This provides a standard for decision making and executing priorities throughout the organization. An employee-centric framework results in a consistent operating vision that is centered around the impact on your employees, customers, then stakeholders.

Depending on the severity of your current situation, this type of change will result in a significant culture shift. When executed properly, it will have a lasting positive impact on the business. Keep in mind, implementations of this magnitude can be grueling and will likely take time to fully take hold throughout the organization.

Be careful not to fall back into old habits when things get tough. You cannot say that employees are a priority and that you are committed to providing a better work environment, then turn around the next quarter end and mandate that employees work 14-hour days for seven days straight to meet the quarter. Nothing will demotivate employees quicker than hearing their senior leaders say one thing when the actions they live daily say the complete opposite.

Your obligation to your employees must be more than a mission statement. Avoid taking action based solely on what seems to be politically expedient. Every initiative you launch and action you take should be done because you believe that is what is in the best interest of the organization and the people you employ. Taking the path of least resistance will never work as you will ultimately lose the trust of your team.

ACQUIRING CONSTANT FEEDBACK

Most companies have some sort of annual survey process. The companies on the forefront of truly embracing the employee experience recognize that this annual data collection method is not nearly enough. If you are gathering data only once per year, you are missing a lot. Depending on the circumstances, asking the same questions in March may produce drastically different results than if asked in August.

Would you collect operational data only once per year? Just think about it. If only once per year you received a report that told you the productivity of your plant, the number of units you shipped, your on-time delivery rate, how could you then develop a plan to improve for the upcoming year? You can see where I am headed; that would be absurd. You cannot have a meaningful discussion or an impactful plan with data that is irrelevant by the time you receive it.

The same principle applies to employee engagement. Remember, people have an innate need to be seen, heard, and appreciated. Your team is no different. Annual surveys are a snapshot of time. The results are influenced by the work environment or situation immediately preceding the survey. Priorities, attitudes, and opinions change; so, waiting an entire year to determine if you are on track is wasting precious time. The more frequently you collect feedback, the better chance you have of capturing the true undercurrent of the organization and planning actions accordingly.

PAVE YOUR OWN PATH

Your company may choose to complete a survey only once a year. You, on the other hand, must be gathering data year-round. You need to have a firm understanding of what your employees are saying and the emotions they are experiencing.

Think about it as a continuous feedback loop. This way when situations pop up that have a negative impact on your team's engagement you are not only aware but are able to quickly take corrective action. This responsiveness mitigates issues before performance is affected.

If David's leader had been actively seeking feedback, do you think he could have helped David remain engaged? What about Chelsey, could she have been retained?

When it comes to addressing challenges, it is crucially important that you include your team in any resolution decision. Do not assume you know how to fix their problem or that the solution you come up with will be the right one. You need to be aware of the current challenge and empower your team to help identify a resolution.

People leaders do not waste their time chasing arbitrary survey metrics because they collect constant feedback. This information provides the insight needed for them to take the necessary measured action that enables peak performance from their team. Managers often struggle to grasp this concept. The idea of taking action but not measuring the impact seems counterproductive to those who are tactically focused and metrics driven.

Unfortunately, many companies and managers execute engagement as simply a check the box activity.

- ✓ Get the survey results
- ✓ Review the survey results
- ✓ Choose the low-hanging fruit to work on for the year
- ✓ Create an action plan
- ✓ Submit an action plan
- ✓ DONE

These same companies struggle to understand why their annual engagement scores and metrics are not improving. Meaningful change comes from taking ownership of the results. Success follows executing continuous improvement actions based on the employee feedback obtained.

TAKE MEANINGFUL ACTION

Action plans are great tools for ensuring alignment, providing visibility, and driving accountability; however, everything does not belong on an action plan. You do not get credit for doing the basics.

Given your role and responsibilities, some things are just standard operating procedures; therefore, they don't belong in your action plan. You are expected to do them with or without an action plan. For example, you should be holding one on one meetings with each individual on your team. That is a given. It does not belong in an action plan.

Your action plan is your commitment to your team and organization. The items that you place on your action plan absolutely must be delivered and meaningful results produced. Otherwise, you are simply wasting everyone's time and energy on a check-the-box activity. Action plans should be treated as living, breathing documents. This way as new complex issues arise you can easily add them to the plan, dedicate resources to resolving the issue(s), and initiate significant sustainable actions.

When you are constantly getting a pulse check of your team and resolving challenges quickly, you will see the fruits of that effort bear out during the company's next traditional annual survey. Even more importantly, you will begin to feel the difference in your team's work environment. Conflict will decrease, productivity will increase, and your team will be more open to providing you with additional ongoing feedback as they will see and experience the changes that you have made.

EVERY ACTION COUNTS

While every action you take will not end up on an action plan, every action you take is important. Do not forget the simple things. People leaders understand the art of simple yet meaningful interactions. Taking the time to get to know each of your team members personally will enable you to have stronger and more trusting relationships.

By understanding where your employee comes from, what behavior characteristics are based on unique life experiences, and what motivates that individual you will be able to truly fully appreciate who the person is. Knowing someone at this level will make it easier to empathize, communicate, and lead with caring.

Simple awareness of employee engagement is not enough. You must fully comprehend the holistic employee experience journey. Appreciate the impact it has on every aspect of your business. Real results derive from real change.

The culture of teams and organizations is driven by the standards by which the business operates. Treating your employees as internal customers will elevate that vital relationship status. With an increased level of importance placed on internal interactions, you are empowering true change to take hold and thrive. You are laying the foundation that mutual trust and respect can be built upon.

41

3

TRUST - BUILD IT AND KEEP IT!

<u>TRUST = RESPECT AND BOTH MUST BE EARNED</u>

Engagement surveys held annually often highlight one critical outage across people leadership ranks and that is *trust*. Leaders at all levels tend to struggle understanding why employees do not trust them. The concept of trust is understandably a touchy one. Everyone wants to be trusted. I have yet to meet a leader who is okay with being viewed as untrustworthy by their employees.

As a child, you are taught to respect and trust authority figures without question. They are considered to be inherently good. It is believed that these individuals will always protect you and look out for your best interests. These fundamental

43

viewpoints held as children change as we mature into adulthood.

As adults, our perspectives and behaviors toward authority figures often digress. It is expected that others, regardless of authority, will work to earn our trust. The ability and willingness to extend trust becomes dependent on the interactions and experiences shared with that individual.

This guarded approach to managing relationships means that many of your employees no longer give respect and trust freely. Leaders are rarely given the benefit of the doubt. Once you acknowledge this reality, you can devise a plan to improve the relationship you have with your team. This will require you to make efforts to earn the trust of each individual on your team.

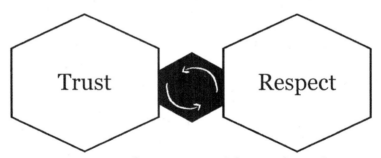

You cannot have one without the other.

As a leader, you are not entitled to either.

Both must be earned.

With trust comes respect; both are explicitly tied together. You cannot have one without the other. If trust or respect have yet to be earned, the best you will get out of your employees is a little common decency. Employees can work for you without particularly liking you. There is no rule that states employees must grant these benefits to their boss in order to receive a paycheck.

As a leader, you need to know that you are not entitled to either. Your goal is to earn the trust and respect of those around you. This includes individuals on your team. Simply having a nice office and a title will not sway opinions or earn you trust. In many cases, this will actually impede the relationship you have with your employees.

Adults naturally gravitate towards people they can relate to. If your employees feel there are no similarities between you, they will be less accepting of your efforts to build a relationship. This is especially true when your employees do not have ample opportunities to interact with you on a personal level. Your employees evaluate each one-on-one interaction to determine the level of trust that you will be granted. Remember: Trust is built on interactions.

11 RULES TO BUILDING AND MAINTAINING TRUST

There are some basic rules to follow to build and maintain the trust of your team:

1. *Be seen* - No one trusts someone they do not know or rarely see. Leaders who are not actively present in the daily actions of their team will experience severe negative consequences. The most damning to any team is the undercurrent of conspiracy theories, especially when tough decisions are made. Shy of an explanation and a trusting relationship, employees will fill the gaps with their own opinions or stories of what is happening and why.

2. *Do what you say you are going to do* - Your commitment is your promise to take action and that is important. If you make promises that you frequently cannot keep, your team will conclude that you are blowing smoke. They will stop asking you for your assistance. Or worse, they will simply disregard anything you say. When situations arise that conflict with a previous commitment, you must immediately inform your team. Being transparent about the change upfront will decrease the back-end water cooler talk later.

3. *Don't commit team member(s) without at least asking them* - There are times when action needs to be taken by someone on your team and there are limited alternative options; so, they really do not have a choice. That being said, no one likes being told what to do. After all, they are adults, not children. Employees enjoy having some level

of control over their work. Taking the time to explain the situation and get their buy-in is critical.

This additional effort on your part will show your team that their opinions matter. Simply providing the employee with a voice and listening to their concerns may not change the situation. Showing you care about how they feel in the given situation will change the way in which they receive and manage the situation.

4. *No job is beneath you* - There are times when you need to jump in and physically help out. After all, you are a part of the team. If your team is working late to meet a deadline, you need to be there. Sitting in your office may show moral support, but that is not what your team wants from you. They need you to be actively helping them get the work done. Showing your team that you are willing to jump in and do what it takes to help out will build your team's confidence in you as a leader. Using your actions to show the team that you care about what they are going through and that you are with them 100% is one of the easiest ways to develop trust.

5. *Mind your tone* - How you communicate information matters greatly to how it is received. There is a stark difference between the way managers and People Leaders communicate a task to someone on their team. Managers will often dictate a task as a demand, "You need to get the

invoices processed by Friday." Whereas a people leader will offer a friendlier, more cooperative tone, "We need to get the invoices processed by Friday. Do you think you can handle it or may I help you get them in?"

The tone you choose to use will have a direct impact on the results you receive. There are three types of employees when it comes to communication. There are some employees who are motivated by tough talk. There are those who completely shut down when spoken to harshly. The least desirable are the employees who could not care less about what you say or how you say it; they are just working for a paycheck. Yelling may be acceptable in the sports world; it is unproductive and completely inappropriate in the business environment no matter the circumstance.

6. *Give credit where credit is due* - Never take credit for the team's success. You have the benefit of a great team around you. Their work enables you to achieve your goals and objectives. When things go well and recognition is awarded, never forget that you are not the one who deserves the accolades. Your team absolutely is. This works in two ways.

The first line of business is ensuring that your team feels appreciated for their work. Do not assume they know how you feel. You will need to express gratitude in a way that is appropriate for the individuals on your team. The second action necessary is providing visibility to your team and their efforts. When sitting in a leadership meeting and you receive positive feedback, take the time to say, "Thank you, the team worked really hard to make this happen. I will pass your message along to them." Or you could take it one step further and request the individual providing the compliment send a quick email to the team thanking them directly.

7. *Never trickle-down blame* - If your team misses a deadline or someone makes a mistake, you own it. That is one of the perks (pun intended) of being the leader. Public shaming of an employee is never appropriate. Nor should you allow any other leader to exhibit this behavior towards someone on your team. Perceptions are easily swayed. One mistake should not forever damn an employee.

A good leader understands that you never pass the blame along to your employees. Your responsibility in this situation is to protect your team from external forces. Simultaneously, you are quietly working to ensure the error does not happen again. This often means sitting in a leadership meeting being pummeled by the arrows your counterparts are throwing at you. While it is not enjoyable to be in that situation, you must not allow the lack of cohesion and bad behavior to leave that room. It must never reach your employees.

8. *Be honest* – Sometimes, as a leader, you must ask your team to work long hours or complete a project that will be unpopular. Approaching your team with honesty will go a long way. If you know that what you are about to ask of them will be a miserable undertaking, just be honest and say it. "I have been asked to pull this project forward by two weeks. I know how much I am asking, but I could really use your help on this one." Trying to dress things up to make them not seem quite so bad only reinforces the idea that you are out of touch. Employees may not like the situation, but it is much easier to swallow when you are just honest upfront.

9. *Admit mistakes* - When issues come up and mistakes are made, as the team leader you must own them. No excuses or justifications needed. Your team does not expect a long dissertation on why a mistake happened. Nor do they care. Employees just want to know that you are self-aware and humble enough to own when you make mistakes. If you choose not to own up to your mistakes, you are creating a culture where others feel it is acceptable behavior as well. Having a team of people who will not be honest when they make a mistake is a disaster waiting to happen. Leading by example with honesty is crucial to reinforce the character traits you expect your team to follow.

10. *Encourage and enable feedback* - As a People Leader, you want your team to feel comfortable coming to you with ideas, concerns, and feedback. This may be related to their work, their peers, or you as their leader. The way in which you handle yourself during these conversations will determine if they continue over time. You cannot make improvements or fix problems that you do not know exist. Keeping the feedback loop open will be highly beneficial to your team in the long run.

Simply stating that you have an open-door policy is not adequate. Most employees do not feel comfortable just dropping by their boss's office. This is especially true if the topic they want to discuss may be taken as negative. You may need to take opportunities during your one-on-one meetings to actively engage and solicit specific feedback. Providing similar opportunities more casually over lunches or during team meetings will help your team feel comfortable broaching these types of subjects.

11. *Do not be a number chaser* - To maintain credibility within your team, you must not behave in a way that would suggest efforts you are taking are for your own gain. Your employees will know if you are simply trying to improve your own metrics or get out ahead of an upcoming annual survey. Genuine leadership comes from caring. You need to trust that if you do what is right for

your people, from a place of caring, the numbers will follow.

IT'S NOT EASY

It is hard to build trust and even harder to maintain it. The truth is it only takes one misstep to have your team questioning whether you deserve their trust. Two missteps and you are done. You will quickly go from not being trusted to not being trustworthy.

Perceptions are reality. Through that lens, you must understand your intentions are irrelevant. If you have damaged the trust with someone on your team, take some time to evaluate what actions you took to cause the disconnect. Then you must follow through by developing a plan for getting the relationship back on track. Trust is not rebuilt organically. You will have to work at it over time. However, your effort must be substantial in the eyes of the employee.

Trust builds as your actions continuously display that your positive behavior is not a "sometimes" sort of thing. Followership is attained as others see that the well-being of your employees remains front and center as you evaluate every decision coming at you. As trust grows between you and your employees, you will gain their respect. This confidence in you as a leader will be the foundation you build upon as you strive to enable your team to be highly fulfilled and engaged.

Gaining the trust and respect of your team will take time. Maintaining those relationships is even more challenging and demands constant dedication. Understand that your team can realize extraordinary success when they trust what you say, respect you as a leader, and feel valued for their contributions.

As we wrap up this section on trust and respect, I want you to expand your thinking beyond just that of how these rules apply to your team. These same rules can be applied to other relationships as well. As we move into the next chapter, we are going to discuss a key partnership you need and why it may be the most important professional relationship you have.

4

KEY PARTNERSHIP

Halfway through a workday event complete with fun, laughter, and team building, the door opens. It's a full-blown enemy invasion! The air is sucked out of the room and everyone goes completely silent and stares as Eva & Ike approach to join the festivities. What horrible atrocity had they committed to earn such a reaction? Eva & Ike both serve as the department's HR representatives.

You may laugh at how silly it sounds, but do you find yourself a bit standoffish when it comes to discussing department business within earshot of anyone from HR? You're not alone. Human Resources is most often considered a necessary evil, and in some cases, they are even viewed as the enemy.

This characterization is far from accurate when it comes to most HR employees, but as an HR person myself, I have to own that these perceptions exist. Before we can progress our leadership conversation on to the key processes that directly impact your success, we have to deal with the fact that you can't get there alone nor should you have to.

Understand that HR can play a bigger, more impactful role than they are likely playing today. We are going to start with the basics. HR is there for you. It may not always feel that way, but they are. Just to play devil's advocate, because I know this hasn't been the experience for many leaders, let's say you feel like you have the worst HR person ever who has never helped you with a single thing. You likely can't figure out exactly what he/she does all day, except for making your life miserable, of course.

Instead of assuming the worst or complaining about what you are not getting, try to figure out what the performance objectives are for the HR team. That one critical piece of information will tell you exactly what your HR partner should be working on. You may not agree with these objectives, but it will give you perspective and allow you to have a more meaningful conversation about the needs and expectations you have.

In my experience, conflict often occurs because no one has taken the time to attempt and build a relationship. You know, a relationship with trust and respect, all the stuff we just talked about. So for the purposes of trying something new in an effort to get better results, let's assume that your HR partner wants you to be successful and is willing to help you if you will only allow it.

We have talked about building trust and respect with your team. The same principles apply to HR. Regardless of the situation today, HR should be an active member of your team. This can only occur when you really know your HR partner.

At this moment if you are not sure what your HR partner's strengths and weaknesses are, then you cannot possibly know when or how to utilize them effectively. You must start there, figuring that out first. Until you take that step, you will simply have untapped potential. You are likely not using HR to your best and fullest advantage.

UNTAPPED POTENTIAL

Many managers do not express a high opinion of HR. There is a definite lack of awareness as to the true purpose of Human Resources. Contrary to popular belief, HR is not full of a bunch of paper pushers who enjoy creating new policies to make your life more difficult. Those who have this opinion have no idea what they are missing. Managers who do not appreciate the value of HR tend to have a very narrow understanding of how to best make use of this resource and it shows. Managers will use HR as the process executors.

If you are utilizing HR solely as administrative support, you are hindering your own objectives and sabotaging your own success. The benefits received through these interactions will be equal to the strength of the relationship that you actively maintain. If you only visit HR when you have a dilemma, you are choosing to react to situations instead of avoiding them altogether.

NOT ALL HR RELATIONSHIPS ARE CREATED EQUAL

You may not even be aware of what you are missing if you have not been fortunate enough to collaborate with a strong HR partner in the past. There are generally two types of HR people. Both serve the same purpose, which is to enable the organization's success through its people. The untapped resources of those talented *Resources* remain largely underutilized because management and HR fail to effectively collaborate on a common goal – to drive maximum employee engagement.

There is HR and then there is an HR Partner. While they share a function, that is where the similarities end. Where traditional HR personnel supports the business to enable success, an HR partner collaborates with the business to achieve success.

WHY AN HR PARTNER

True HR partners understand your goals and objectives because they have spent time with you building a strong relationship. They are thoroughly aware of the challenges or barriers you are facing. They fully grasp what you are up against. HR partners are dedicated and well versed in helping you through it. Part of building this relationship is laying the foundation for the rules of engagement. Having this discussion and obtaining alignment early on will avoid confusion or misunderstanding later. Know that your HR Partner will be tough but fair. He or she will have very high expectations for you as a people leader; accordingly, will have no qualms with holding you accountable.

This cohesive dynamic allows you to move fast. You have concise discussions about the topic at hand; quickly evaluate possibilities and move forward with the best available option. Needless delay is avoided if you have someone you trust and really connect with.

There are no limits to what a leader and partner will collaborate on when there is a strong bond between the two. Interactions are no longer restricted to reacting to "HR" problems. Leaders who truly value their HR partners want them at the table for every business decision as there will be an impact felt by employees.

Giving HR a seat at the table gives you a view thru that lens. People Leaders will always have HR there to keep them honest or hold them accountable just to make sure they are thinking through every element. This ensures that they are aware of what the fallout will be, good or bad, as a result of every decision they make.

THIS RELATIONSHIP TAKES WORK

An HR partnership is like any other relationship. Some work organically and some take significant effort. Having the right style fit with your HR Partner will make it much easier and quicker to build the necessary bond. When a Leader and their Partner share the same values, there will be limited conflict when the time comes to tackle the hard issues.

Maintaining a productive relationship with a partner who has a style unlike yours is possible; however, it does require considerable effort from both parties. Those with opposing styles tend to take longer to trust one another. If you are not careful, this lack of trust can bring productivity to a grinding halt as every conversation instigates a debate. When faced with these challenges, remember this is not a battle.

The goal is not to win the conversation. Your goal is to be successful. Rather than dig in, take time to discuss the challenge(s) and options, and most importantly, listen to the feedback you are being offered. Over time, as these challenges are conquered and conversations become cooperative, you will naturally begin building equal confidence in one another. Thus, allowing alignment to be achieved and mutual trust to be formed.

SOAR TO NEW HEIGHTS

Just as every pilot has a wingman, your HR Partner is your wingman. The two of you face all things together with a single purpose. They will support your endeavors, protect you from outside influences, and act in your best interests at all times. Once the rapport is built, you are confident you can come to your HR Partner at any time for anything. Together you can forge a partnership that makes your job easier, produces substantial business results, and improves your capabilities as a leader.

If you have a strong HR Partner today, you know it. If you don't have the relationship with HR that you want and need, now is the time to reach out and start building one. There are, however, a few things about how HR Partners operate that you need to be aware of. Understanding these core traits will help you level set your expectations and avoid surprises.

HR PARTNERS (WHAT GOOD LOOKS LIKE)

- Fundamentally care about all employees
- Will fight with you, if necessary, to protect the company and its employees
- Put the needs of the organization above their own aspirations
- Understand the company goals and where they can help achieve them
- Do what is right, always
- Speak the truth, even when it is not popular
- Will push you to be a better leader
- Will question your decisions to validate that you have thought through every potential impact
- Tackle challenges head-on
- Will hold you and others accountable for the actions and behaviors exhibited
- Remind you of the commitments you have made and the importance of keeping them
- Are often nonconventional in their approach to driving culture change
- Always look to identify a win-win in any situation
- Are not afraid to venture into unknown territory
- Are fully dedicated to the success of others, including you

DYNAMIC LEADERSHIP

~ PROCESS ~

How Talent Management executional excellence drives growth.

There are six core processes that make up the function of Talent Management. Each talent process is interconnected. To be successful, you must execute each with excellence. This book will go through each process, from Recruiting through Offboarding, from beginning to end as though you were getting ready to hire a new team member. However, that is not actually where the process starts.

Constant evaluation of your organizational health is critical to continued business growth and long-term success. Succession planning is the foundation that determines what actions are required any time there is a vacancy. Below you will find the Talent Management Cycle to highlight how each core process relates to the others.

TALENT MANAGEMENT CYCLE OVERVIEW

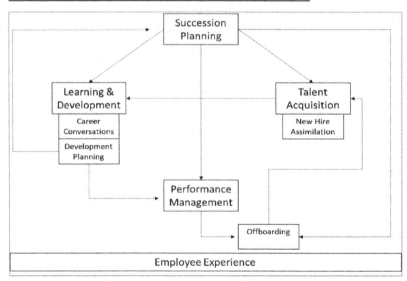

We will get into the details of how succession planning works and why it is the most important of the Talent Management processes a bit later. To get you started, it is important to think about the questions that you must ask yourself as a leader with regards to the talent health of your organization. Asking these questions prior to a vacancy allows you to plan and execute strategically and avoid reactionary bad decisions.

After taking a moment to review the Talent Management flow chart on the next page, get ready to move from *People* and *Individual Relationships* that we covered in the first half of the book to *Process* and *Teams*. It is here that you will find best practices and tools. We kick off this journey with Talent Acquisition. Even if you think you are a pro, don't be tempted to skip this chapter. A hiring mistake is a costly one that isn't easy to rectify.

TALENT MANAGEMENT CYCLE – FLOW CHART

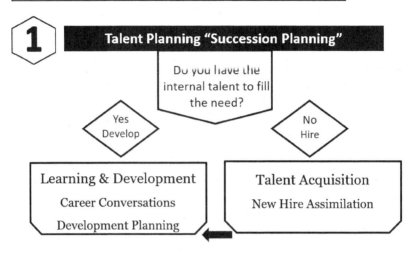

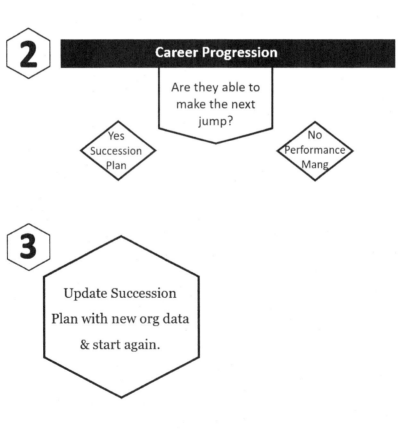

5

TALENT ACQUISITION

Talent Acquisition or recruiting, as an activity, is either loved or hated by hiring managers. In all my years specializing in Talent, here is what I can tell you: Managers hate talent acquisition. It takes time, energy, and resources away from what they believe are their core objectives. Some of the main complaints that managers have include: "The process, itself, takes too long." "I can't find the right candidate." "I don't have time." With very few exceptions, I would argue that if the process is that painful, then you are doing something wrong. As you make the transition from tactical manager to strategic leader, you will find there is tremendous value in the recruiting process when executed effectively.

People leaders have a tendency to thoroughly enjoy the hiring process for a variety of reasons. The recruiting process is viewed as an opportunity. Consequently, it is not considered a burden or a drain on resources. Some enjoy talking directly to candidates, looking for the diamond in the rough, using the opportunity to think about what their future organization could be.

Regardless of the specific reason why they enjoy it, hiring managers who are strong people leaders are always looking for the next leader who:

- Will bring a new skill to the team

- Exhibits a strong desire to help others learn and grow

- Possesses an entrepreneur's spirit and will improve the team's innovative capabilities

As the hiring manager, the speed by which you can fill your role will be dependent on your ability to follow a well-designed recruiting process. If unfocused, you will experience painful delays and costly rework. Every vacancy adds stress to the organization. The longer it takes you to fill it, the greater the impact will be on your currently overloaded team. Their frustration will continually mount as long as the vacancy remains unfilled as they are forced to pick up the slack.

There are five critical phases of the recruiting process: Planning, Intake, Interviewing, Debrief, and Offer. Flawlessly executing each consecutive phase will enable you to avoid simple yet common missteps that will derail your efforts and require you to restart your search from the beginning.

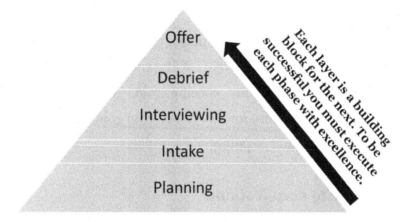

PLANNING

Think of the Planning phase as your foundation. If you do not get this right, everything else will fall apart in time. Let us start with the basics. Yes, you need a Job Description for your role. Yes, you must be the one who writes it.

Out with the old, in with the new

Roles can change significantly over a short period of time. Do not attempt to take the easy path. You cannot just recycle an old job description. To be abundantly clear, if it was written over a year ago it is now old. Think about how much your role has changed in the last year or two. It is highly unlikely that you are still performing the exact same job duties.

This vacancy is an opportunity to change things up. Do you really want someone to do the exact same tasks as the person who left? More importantly, would you like to upgrade and bring in talent with a new skill set that your team is missing?

A well-written Job Description will perform two key functions. It will explain what skills and capabilities are necessary to perform this specific role. Additionally, it provides the opportunity for you to sell your role, your team, and your organization to potential candidates.

Remember to keep it simple

You can call the role whatever you want internally, but when you post your position externally chose a title that makes sense. What would a candidate today be searching for on the job boards? Your job title is not the place to be unique or sentimental. A unique job title will only limit the candidates who see it.

Now that candidates can find your job, you want them to apply or self-select out; thus, ensuring you have the most qualified candidates to view. Candidates today are short on time and patience, causing them to spend a minute or two at best reviewing the job requirements. Your posting needs to get their attention and convince them to do more than just skim the content.

There are two enormous turn-offs for candidates that you need to be aware of when creating your job description:

- A massive laundry list of job requirements that seems unrealistic

- Using internal acronyms with a whole bunch of junk they do not understand.

This is where candidates will self-select out. If you are seeing a low volume of applications, one of these two is likely the reason. Most candidates will not apply to a job where they do not meet most of the job specifications. Therefore, you must be precise in what you consider a requirement versus what is preferred.

There is no award for the longest job description, so only list items that are truly important. Skills that are nice to have but not required can be vetted during the interview process and treated as a bonus, not as a restriction. You do want non-qualified candidates to opt out of the process when they do not possess the most critical required qualifications. Even so, you need to avoid losing good candidates because they do not have every box checked.

Remember, where a manager will be focused on a plug-and-play candidate who can immediately execute against the current tasks and deadlines, a people leader has a different approach. People Leaders will hire individuals who have a high capability ceiling with strong future growth potential. The necessary time is then invested to teach the technical and job-specific skills necessary to perform the role.

INTAKE SESSION

The intake session is often skipped as nonessential. What a mistake that turns out to be! Spending a few minutes at this phase will save you big in the interview phase to follow. The intake session ensures that you, your HR Partner, and your recruiter are aligned to exactly what you are looking for in candidates for this position.

Communicate Need

Define Roles

Align Next Actions

The clearer you are upfront, before the process kicks off, the better and more consistent quality of candidates you will see. There is nothing more frustrating than getting weeks into the search only to then find the candidates you are seeing are not what you are really looking for. This only occurs when you have a poorly written job description or your recruiting team lacks alignment with your expectations.

The sample Intake Session template will help you ensure that there is clarity in what you are looking for. It also clearly delineates who on the team is responsible to complete which actions.

Sample: Intake Session Template

INTAKE SESSION								
Position Title			Requisition Number				Date	
Hiring Manager		Email				Work Phone		
HR Partner		Email				Work Phone		

GENERAL INFORMATION								
Annual Salary		Bonus Target		Signing Bonus		Other		
Relocation Assistance		Visa Sponsorship		Primary Work Location		Remote Work Available		
Yes	No	Yes	No			Yes	No	
Level of Education Required		Years of Relevant Work Experience				People Leader Role		
None	2yr	4yr	<2	3-5	6-10	10+	Yes	No

ROLE SPECIFIC INFORMATION
What are the critical qualities that you must see in someone joining your team?
What technical skills, product knowledge, or industry experience is required for this position?
What is the specific scope of responsibility for this role?

PHONE SCREEN INTERVIEW INFORMATION			
Name	Title	Email	Phone

ONSITE INTERVIEW TEAM				
	Name	Title	Email	Phone
1				
2				
3				
4				
5				

PHONE SCREENS WILL SAVE YOU TIME & MONEY

If your organization does not have a recruiter or an agency they partner with on recruiting, I strongly recommend that you or someone on your functional team conduct phone screens. HR can assess things like work history and leadership capabilities. Your HR Partner is likely unable to evaluate the candidate's technical knowledge unless considerable time has already been spent supporting your specific function.

Conducting technical phone screenings will ensure that you do not bring candidates onsite who lack the fundamental skills necessary to perform in this position. You will be better served to spend 30 minutes upfront than to bring multiple candidates onsite where you will accrue travel expenses and waste the time of an entire interview team.

FOCUS ON FIT & TECHNICAL CAPABILITIES

A good phone screen should last about 30 minutes. You do not need to learn every detail of the candidate's experience; if they are good, you will learn more in the next round of interviews. You simply need to have a reasonable understanding of the potential fit with your team and the technical capabilities possessed that will enable strong performance in the role. This stage is used to filter out any candidates that do not meet your minimum expectations.

The concept of "fit" can be challenging as additional scrutiny is being placed on this topic. Fit is a common word used in multiple ways throughout the Talent Management process. With regards to interviewing, fit should be viewed as a work execution descriptor.

For example, let's say you have an opening for a Project Manager role to support a new customer-requested product. This customer is highly involved and is constantly changing its mind on even the base requirements. It is not ideal, but the profit margin for this project has the potential to set a company record. You know you need an experienced Project Manager who can quickly change directions, remains flexible, and has a lot of patience. He or she must also operate very well in the gray, as this is a unique situation where the end result and process for getting there is evolving. In this case, when you are looking for fit, you are looking for a candidate who possesses these specific traits. You cannot hire someone who is extremely structured in how they manage projects, as they would not be successful.

I would recommend that you take a moment to define what fit means to you during the interview phase. This will ensure that you are constantly using the same definition and not using it as a catch-all for candidates you don't like. Your definition then needs to be shared with the recruiting team so that the term is used in alignment.

The sample Phone Screen Template provided can help you evaluate the candidate's current skill set, future growth potential, and career aspirations. You will need to determine what additional technical or functional specific questions would be helpful to filter the candidate pool.

Sample: Phone Screen Template

GENERAL INFORMATION		
Candidate Name		
Interview Date	Interview Time	
Position Title		

STANDARD QUESTIONS
Why are you interested in this position?
What skills do you have that will help you be successful in this position?
What responsibilities of this position would be new learning for you?
What type of work do you enjoy most? What type of work are you most passionate about?
Tell me about a time when you achieved results to a goal through others who did not report to you. OR Describe a situation that illustrates when you achieved a goal by utilizing skills in collaboration and influence.
What are your career aspirations (short term & long term)?

PEOPLE LEADER POSITIONS
People Leader - What is the one area that you feel you must develop to be a stronger people leader?
People Leader - In your past roles, how much of your time was spent managing the work vs. managing the people?

It is recommended that you limit your focus of functional specific questions to three or four. This will provide you enough information to enable you to predict how the candidate's level of technical capabilities will compare to what you need in the role.

For example, if you are hiring financial analysts you may want to understand how they have used data to predict an outcome or test their Excel capabilities prior to bringing them onsite. If you are looking for a software engineer, you will likely probe into the technology they are currently familiar with as well as the willingness to learn new solutions moving forward.

CANDIDATE CARE WILL MAKE OR BREAK YOU

Candidate Care is precisely what it sounds like. It is the manner in which you and your team treat a candidate and how they feel about interactions throughout the recruiting process. Job seekers can be much more sensitive and have significantly elevated expectations in a booming job market.

With limited talent availability and an abundance of job opportunities, candidates expect to be treated to a delightful experience. This begins with the initial contact during the phone screen completely through the process. Candidate care does not end until the candidate shows up on the first day as your new hire.

INTERVIEWING

Don't assume you are a good interviewer. It takes time and consistency to hone the skills to truly identify top talent. If you only hire for a role or two every few years, know that you are rusty. If you have not attended an Interviewer Training in the last several years, do it now. It will save you considerable heartache throughout the process. The same principle applies to your interview team.

Select the right interview team

The best interviewers are skilled at assessing talent. Keep this in mind as you build your interview team. Interviewers that come from diverse backgrounds and have varying experiences often provide the best insight into a candidate's background. Above all else, your interviewers must be passionate about hiring top talent into your organization.

Your interview team should *not* be chosen based on who has time available on their calendar. If you believe someone lacks the necessary competence to effectively evaluate top talent, you will not truly rely on the input provided. You should not include this individual in the hiring process. Doing so is a waste of time and energy for both the interviewer and the candidate.

Every person on the interview team should have a defined role that has a purpose. After defining each interviewer's role, you then need to take the extra step of communicating to the interview team exactly which area each is responsible for investigating. This will avoid the duplication of conversations with the candidate. You have a limited amount of time with these candidates. You want to ensure that your interview team gets as much information out of the candidate as possible.

There are three required roles for any interview team:

- Your role as the Hiring Manager is to evaluate the candidate's future potential and ability to acclimate to your team environment. You are looking for a balance between the candidate's ability to operate within the team given the environment today as well as the ability to elevate the team's capabilities for the future.

- Your HR Partner should evaluate the candidate's work history and career aspirations. You will also be made aware of any watch outs or development areas that may be of consequence.

- Other interview team member(s) should be utilized to evaluate the candidate's technical capability.

It should not take an entire committee to help you fill your vacancy. Three to five trusted people is plenty to give you the additional insights necessary to make a wise choice. Anything more than that is overkill and is a turn off to candidates. Interviews should be about gathering relevant information, not wearing candidates down.

Interview etiquette basics

On interview day, show up and put your best foot forward. As busy as you may be, for the next 45 minutes your undivided attention needs to be with the candidate in the room. Shake off any frustrations you may be carrying. It does not matter how long you have been trying to fill the position or how many candidates you have spoken to this week. For this moment, the candidate in the room is the most important person in the world to you.

Make every attempt to avoid the last-minute interview schedule juggle. Not only because it will absolutely drive your HR Partner crazy, but it sends a signal to the candidate that you are messy and unprepared. Remember, in a candidate's mind, it is a candidate's market. So, act like it!

Don't forget to sell

Even the largest, most reputable companies struggle in a tight labor market. You must work harder than ever to close the sale on potential employees. Caveat: Do so honestly. One of the greatest complaints of employees with less than one year of service is that the role is not what they expected it would be. That is an error that originates during the interview process. Own who you are and how you operate. Transparency upfront avoids potential employer remorse for new hires later.

How to Make the Hard Sell and Do It Honestly

I am an interviewer for a Medical Technology company. We operate in a fast-paced environment where the priorities are constantly changing. We lack the standard process that you would expect from a company of our size. I make a point to be fully transparent with all candidates so that they come into employment with us with their eyes wide open. My pitch is the same regardless of the candidate, position, or role level.

"If you are someone who likes to know exactly what you are going to do each day; if you enjoy having a to-do list, get satisfaction from completing those tasks, and believe there should be a standard way to get things done, this is not the place for you. However, if you are someone who really likes the challenge of an ever-changing environment where no two days are the same and you enjoy the challenge of just figuring things out on the fly without a roadmap, you can excel in our environment."

New hires must thrive in your world. You have spent the necessary time evaluating their skill sets and work style preferences during the interview process. You ensure you are choosing the candidate best suited for your team by painting a clear, realistic picture of the working environment and daily operating conditions.

INTERVIEW DEBRIEF

Hiring decisions should never be made in a hallway. You and your interview team need time to discuss the candidate(s) in detail. As quickly following the interview(s) as possible, you should ensure a debrief is scheduled and held.

During the debrief, it is important that you hold your thoughts and opinions until the very end. If you have an inexperienced interview team, your opinion may sway them. Each interviewer should take time to share what was learned and provide a recommendation as to whether the candidate should be hired for the position. Once everyone else has shared their thoughts and feedback, you should do the same. With this holistic view of the candidates under consideration and the recommendations of your interview team, it is time to make the call: Offer or No offer.

Stop looking for Purple Unicorns – they don't exist

Once you have found a good candidate, you need to move quickly. Spending countless weeks continuing the process in the hopes of seeing more resumes only costs you time and talent. Do not take the weekend to think about it. It is highly unlikely that you will change your mind. It just delays the inevitable, opening the door to reviewing just a few more resumes. Before you know it, you have started all over again; only now you have a candidate out there waiting to hear something from you.

It's your Decision – Own It!

Be confident in what you want. Trust your interview team; after all, you chose them for a reason. Now is the time for you to be decisive. It is okay to keep looking if you have not identified a strong candidate. If that is the case, cut the remaining candidates loose.

I have yet to meet a hiring manager who, after keeping a candidate warm for months, moved forward with the hire and ultimately felt comfortable or confident about bringing that individual onboard. These backup candidates generally carry an asterisk next to their name as the one who got here because there was no other option. Thankfully, these situations are rare. Generally, candidates sit in the maybe pile for months on end only to eventually get the not-so-personal regret letter.

It is important to remember that candidates talk about their experiences with their friends, family, and basically anyone who reads a post in today's world of social media. Keep in mind that even if this individual does not join your organization, he or she could still be a potential customer or consumer. Do not let your company image and reputation be tarnished by a poor interview experience. It is not easy to overcome negative public relations stories; just avoid it. The easiest way to circumvent these situations is to make the decision, then move on.

Immediately following the debrief, align with your HR Partner on the offer details if the decision is to extend an offer. Get the offer letter out as soon as possible. Keep in mind if you think highly enough of the candidate to make an offer for your role, there is likely another employer out there hoping to do the same.

AVOID THE BLACK HOLE

Most organizations have a habit of working extremely hard to get the acceptance then dial back the efforts until closer to the candidate's start date. This is what candidates and new employees refer to as the "Black Hole." For a soon-to-be new hire, there is nothing worse than a company making you an offer, getting you excited about this next chapter of your life, and then nothing ... crickets.

In many cases, it could be months before new hires physically show up onsite. Keeping them engaged is part of your job as the hiring manager. When you get busy and start reprioritizing your list of critical things to get done, remember your New Hire has not started yet. It is likely that he or she is still being contacted and pursued by recruiters as well as other companies. Do not leave the door open unnecessarily. If you think the process has been painful to get to this point, just wait until a candidate feels no one cares enough to pay attention and decides to back out at the 11th hour.

If you are thinking of delegating this task to your HR Partner, don't. Candidates have no desire at this point to hear from HR. They want to talk directly to you. Remember, it could be an extended period of time before your candidate arrives onsite. The interactions between you during this time are critical to delivering excellent Candidate Care. These conversations will provide the soon-to-be new hire valuable information that enables the two of you to begin building a relationship.

During these conversations, your New Hire will be seeking information about what:

- A day in the life is really like

- They will be working on

- The team is like

Interviewing, as an action, is a simple task. Mastering the ability to assess talent, that is much more difficult. It is a skill that can be developed and improved over time. For more information on Recruiting and Interviewing training, contact your Human Resources Partner to see what internal courses or materials are available.

6

NEW HIRE ASSIMILATION

BEFORE THEY ARRIVE

It is getting close to the time for your New Hire to show up. Spend some time ensuring that you are ready for the arrival of your newest team member. This section will walk you through the standards, processes, and requirements for creating an assimilation plan. These resources will support your efforts to effectively onboard your New Hire into the organization.

First things first, check with your HR Partner to see if there is a standard onboarding plan or toolkit available. This information will ensure that everything is in order upon your New Hire's arrival. Have a discussion with your soon-to-be w hire to align on his or her official start date. Be sure to communicate the agreed-upon start date to your HR Partner so that all necessary paperwork is processed accordingly.

A member of the Human Resources team will generally manage the arrangements and communications with the new hire around the attendance of New Hire Orientation. When possible, you want to schedule your New Hire to start on or near the date of the New Hire Orientation. It is during this session that your New Hire will complete all necessary paperwork, learn about the relevant company policies, and obtain benefits information.

Pre-schedule what is important

Pre-schedule all introductory meetings with key members of your team and key cross-functional peers with whom your New Hire will collaborate on a frequent basis. The earlier you can get it on the calendar the better. Holding this time with employees will ensure that you are not scrambling later to help your New Hire make these critical connections.

Verify and enroll your New Hire in all required training needed to enable your New Hire a successful start. You will want to spread the training over the first 30 to 60 days so that your New Hire has time to digest the information while gradually taking on more work. Avoid delaying training. Once your New Hire is working at full capacity, it will be extremely difficult to dedicate the necessary time to complete the training. While new hire training is important, providing your

New Hire the necessary time to focus on pre- and post-work is equally important. Be sure to schedule a time to review post-course to discuss what new learning was acquired during the training session and how the knowledge can be applied in daily actions.

Sample: Required Training

Timing	Training Topic	Course Description	Learning Objective	Contact
Day 1	Safety Training	Factory and site safety requirements	How to remain safe while visiting the warehouse	Health & Safety Manager
Week 1	Ride Along	Customer Site Visit	How our customers interact with our products	John Smith
Week 2	ABC System	The system used to track customer calls	How to effectively use the system	Jane Jones

Ensure that you have the necessary tools available when your New Hire arrives. Do not forget the basics. It does not say much for your leadership capabilities for your New Hire to show up without having a desk or a computer ready when they arrive. Check with your HR Partner to see if there is a standard checklist to help you manage the process.

NOW YOUR NEW HIRE IS HERE

Your job is to make the transition from candidate experience to employee experience seamless. It should feel like one smooth process. New employees will determine if they made the right decision within their first 90 days. If at any point during that time they question why they joined your company, you are in trouble. They may stick around a bit longer for their resume's sake, but once they make the decision that they made a mistake you will not be able to get them back; they will have one foot out the door.

Ensure that your New Hire does not have any second guesses or regrets. You will need to be present, engaged, and available. Do not take off on any trips during your New Hire's first 30 days, if possible. You will want to check in frequently with your New Hire. This does not need to be a formally scheduled meeting. Just make a point to swing by to see how things are going.

Provide a Key Resource List

It is helpful to provide new hires a contact list of who they should contact when they have questions based on the topic or tool. Employees who are still learning often do not want to ask a lot of questions of their direct supervisor. To avoid any anxious feelings about their lack of knowledge or insecurities about needing additional help, simply instruct them to reach out to the experts directly with any questions. Just remember that you still need to remain engaged and available should your New Hire have questions or need additional help.

Be sure to get your New Hire connected to other recent arrivals. Starting at a new company can be overwhelming. It is important for employees to have a support system of other people who are currently experiencing a similar situation. Building this community early will help them make the transition. It is especially critical if you have a new hire joining your team directly from college or one who has relocated as part of this employment. A network provides an additional layer of support to help the new hires work through any concerns they may have or challenges that they may be experiencing.

Sample: Contact List

Name	Email	Resource For
Jane Smith	janesmith@abc.com	IT - System issues, company phone
John Doe	johndoe@abc.com	Company card, Travel Policy, and booking Company car
HR Partner	HRpartner@abc.com	Your HR Partner, for anything you need
New Hire Buddy	NewHire@abc.com	Questions about the team or location

Additionally, all new hires will need a list of the standing meetings that they are expected to attend. This should inform them of when the meeting will be held, where the meeting takes place, a description of the meeting purpose, and who leads the meeting. Over time, you may want to elaborate by adding a section that outlines the expectations you have of your New Hire during these meetings. For example, will you be expecting your New Hire to present updates? If so, you will need to provide guidance as to how and when those updates should occur.

Sample: Standing Meetings

Meeting Title	Time & Date	Description	Leader Name
Operations Call	Mondays 9-10 a.m. EST	Weekly preview of orders	John Smith
HR - Team Meeting	Tues & Thurs 8-8:30 a.m. EST	An in-person meeting to discuss current open positions	HR Director
1:1 Meeting	Every other Wed. 2-3 p.m. EST	Time for us to catch up	New Hire Name

Don't forget about the technology that is frequently used internally. Your New Hire will need a list of commonly used technology systems and key intranet links. Providing this information during assimilation will help to cut down on confusion and avoid wasting time searching for information unnecessarily. The sooner your new hires receive access to required information and resources, the more quickly they will become productive.

Sample: Web Resource List

Site	Purpose	URL
Intranet	Where all internal documents are stored	internal-abc.com
Team Site	Where functional documents are shared and stored	engineering-abc.com
Other	Why	Where

SET THEM UP FOR SUCCESS

Do not drop them in the deep end and expect them to swim. Overcoming the chaos of the organization is not a rite of passage. It is just sloppy management. It likely did not feel good when it happened to you, so do not feel the need to pass the tradition along. Level set your expectations. For most new hires, it will take them 90-120 days to get their bearings.

Level loading your new hires' work for the first few months will help build their confidence. If you take it too easy on them, they will get bored. If you give them too much, they will be overwhelmed. Pay attention to non-verbal cues when evaluating their capacity levels. Are they in the office late? Do they seem stressed or confused? These signs may suggest that you need to adjust your new hires' load temporarily.

New hires are sometimes reluctant to say "no" or to be transparent about their capacity restrictions. You are better off asking them to tell you once they have the hang of things and are ready to take on more. You will find that most new hires will work hard to get up to speed as quickly as possible.

They are often encouraged and excited when able to ask you for more. When they do approach you, be prepared. Know what the next item or task is that you want them to learn. Before throwing something else their way, take a moment to acknowledge the job they are doing and the effort they are putting in. Do not underestimate the value of a little simple reassurance. "You are doing a great job" or "I appreciate how hard you are working to get to know the team," whatever it is, say it. They need to hear it.

Perspective is important here. While it may take up to 120 days for your new hires to get their feet under them, it will take even longer for them to become truly independent. Understanding the traditional learning cycle and looking for opportunities to accelerate that learning will improve your New Hire's confidence and capability. In the early days, you will want to be very clear in the tasks that your New Hire needs to complete while providing specific instructions for how to complete it. As your new hires grow their knowledge, you should begin to offer them more opportunities to experiment and lead on their own.

Taking the time early for your new hires to try and fail while in a safe space will be crucial in their development. If done with proper management support, this practice of experiment and fail safely can propel your new hires' careers. They are getting constant opportunities to learn, grow, and evolve much earlier in their careers than most.

INTERNAL TRANSFERS NEED LOVE, TOO

As hiring managers, we often forget that when someone is transferring to a new role they need attention as well. While an internal employee likely has the necessary skills and competencies needed to perform the role, we cannot assume that they can jump in on day one and hit the ground running.

You should treat internal transfers as if they are new hires until you see solid and consistent examples of them being able to perform in their roles independently. Understand that each team functions uniquely. Your transfer will need to learn how the team operates and where he or she plays in the new dynamics. Time will be needed for acclimation to the new environment.

EXPECT FRUSTRATION

Keep in mind that an internal transfer will experience similar emotions when joining a new team as someone from outside of the organization; however, often these emotions can be heightened.

Employees who were previously at the top of their game and considered experts in their field often have a hard time adjusting to a new role. Going from being highly sought after for your unique skills to now learning new skills where answers are not already known can be a very difficult transition for some to manage. Employees new to their role often experience not only a high level of frustration with the gaps in their capabilities, but also the pace at which they learn.

While you are expected to stay connected and spend time with all new members of your team, you may find it helpful to assign transfers with a coach from your current team. The coach's role is to answer any questions the new members may have, to point them in the right direction when they need guidance, to be an ear and offer encouragement when the new member is frustrated, as well as to be an advocate to help the new member overcome any challenges.

It will be important for you to maintain perspective. Allow your new member time to grow and develop in this new role. It is not unusual for us to have high expectations of our internal transfers as we have seen them deliver in other capacities. It just can't be expected from day one in their new role.

TRANSITION PLAN

Developing a solid plan for what work the transferring employees can take on immediately and what responsibilities they will pick up over time is tremendously helpful. A transition plan will help everyone feel comfortable with the learning expectations over the coming months. This plan will show new employees that there is not an expectation that they know everything right now. They should be afforded the time to truly learn their new roles. These simple changes to the current internal transfer process will eliminate unnecessary pressure felt by employees. At the same time, it encourages them to really make their mark when they are ready.

To the extent possible, you need to limit the amount of overlap between the employee's former role and the new role. It is unfair to expect people to do their old role while trying to learn their new one. The truth is their performance will suffer for it. The best-laid transition plans rarely get executed on time. As the weeks turn to months, you run the risk of burnout for transitioning employees. It is your job as their new leader to protect them from these situations.

COMMUNICATION BUILDS STRONG FOUNDATIONS

Whether your New Hire is joining your organization for the first time or if he or she is transferring from another department, you must put in the work to build and maintain a strong relationship with the newest member of your team. Communication is the foundation of that relationship.

Depending on the size of your team, it can take a while to truly get to know your people, but the effort must be there. Before you begin evaluating the new hires' capabilities, take the time to get to know who they are and how they operate. During your reoccurring 1:1 meetings, spend time learning about their backgrounds, what makes them tick, and what drives them.

Having this foundational knowledge will help you devise a plan for addressing any capability gaps moving forward. It will also allow you to capture important information about your New Hire that you will want to remember moving forward. If my manager does not remember that I have four children after many conversations where they are mentioned, I will assume that at best he is not a good listener or at worst he just does not care.

You can use the sample 1:1 form provided to keep track of the conversations you have with your team. This allows you to capture important information that you will likely need to reference at some point in the future. Simply complete the form during or immediately after the meeting, keeping a running log over time. Then prior to your next meeting you can check back with your notes to see what you previously discussed.

Remember: You should be spending a few minutes during each 1:1 meeting just getting to know your people and how they are doing. Asking about someone's weekend will not take that much of your time. It can provide you powerful insights into your employees and what they consider important. Not to mention it just makes you seem a bit more human.

Templates are available for download at: fergusonlearning.com/Resources

Sample: One-on-one Tracking Form

Team Member:	Date:
Personal (Spouse, Children, Pets, Hobbies, History, etc.)	
How are things going?	
Team Member Update	
Manager Update (Positive/corrective feedback, follow-up on commitments, delegation, organizational messages)	
Future (Career Discussion/Development Progress Review)	
What support do you need from me?	
Anything I can do better or differently? Anything I should stop doing?	

7

SUCCESSION PLANNING & BUILDING A LEADERSHIP BENCH

YOUR TALENT BENCH IS YOUR RESPONSIBILITY

As a leader, building your talent bench is critical. At some point, you will want to move to a new opportunity yourself. A key enabler of that move is having identified and developed your replacement. Your primary goal is to prepare him or her for the challenge of backfilling you. This preparation will ensure the teams' stability once you are gone. A team's ability to function cannot be dependent on the leader who currently holds the seat. If you move to a new role and the organization falls apart in your absence, you have failed them.

Succession Planning can be challenging. It is like playing a game of checkers and chess at the same time. You must be flexible and responsive to any situation that may come at you, from someone leaving unexpectedly to your organization announcing your entire department will be restructured. In these cases, you are thinking quickly on your feet to react to the situation and address any issues that are presented. Both examples produce a response that is reactionary if you are not thoughtful and intentional.

Simply reacting to a situation is not the preferred method of strong leaders. Leaders want to be prepared and ready for all options; they play chess. They have a defined plan but know a hundred different ways that plan could change and what to do when that inevitable situation unfolds.

You need to start by evaluating each member of your team. This will include their strengths across skill sets and any current capability gaps. Evaluating your employee's potential over the next five years can be a bit more challenging. You are projecting in the future to determine if the employee can continue to develop in order to achieve the next level. Things like agility are given prominent importance. Is the employee willing and able to move to other positions, departments, or locations if necessary?

The subjective nature of evaluating employee potential does carry some risks. You should not assume to know what an employee would or would not be willing to do in the future. Assumptions can be very costly mistakes, but they are completely avoidable. If you are not sure if an employee would be willing to relocate, pointedly ask. You should never restrict an employee's career mobility without data to support your decision.

With all your data collection complete, you now move towards creating a realistic plan that can be executed against. Your plan will need to outline the specific actions necessary to ensure that your employee is ready for the new opportunity when it presents itself. If your employee misses out on an opportunity to advance because there are still areas that need to be developed, that is on you. It is your job to make sure your staff is ready.

Evaluate what you have

Look at the bigger picture

Outline Next Actions

These three steps are each equally important. You cannot develop a solid plan without first conducting a thorough evaluation that provides you strong understanding of the talent you have. You cannot fairly evaluate an employee's capabilities or aspirations if you do not actually speak with him or her. Armed with the performance and potential data you have gathered about the individuals on your team, you can now step back to look at the bigger picture. What is the talent health of your team? Where do you have holes to fill? What actions do you need to take to fill the holes in your team's talent depths?

It is important that you do not shortchange the process of succession planning. If you do, the organization will be forced to live with the consequences of a talent bench that is less than adequate. While this may seem like a lot to undertake, that is just the planning piece.

When it comes to execution, you must be methodical and operate with urgency. A plan alone is useless. You have to show that you can execute your vision. In doing so, the organization needs to experience some improvement or benefit in some way. Strong people leaders are aware of the value that succession planning and execution can bring to their team.

These leaders take the time to work through this process not because it is mandatory but because they know it will holistically improve the results of the team. This process, if done properly, will ensure that you are not surprised by unfolding situations. Yes, Succession Planning is a lot of work and it changes constantly as the organization is always changing. Understand that developing your talent bench is your responsibility and must be one of your top priorities.

No People Leader Is Exempt

Every people leader, regardless of level, should have a well-defined succession plan for their team. When talent planning is restricted to execution at only the most senior levels of the organization, you will run the significant risk of not having a sufficient long-term talent pipeline. The leadership talent you will need 5-10 years from now is likely sitting very deep in your organization.

By teaching all people leaders to think about talent in this way, you are ensuring the viability of your organization in the future. Evaluate the health of your organizational talent by first asking these fundamental questions:

What are the critical roles within my team?

Which roles are necessary stepping-stones to advancing in the organization?

Which roles could be a direct successor to my position?

Evaluation of critical roles and people must be conducted separately. This will avoid you having one person with five different options as their next assignment. We all love our utility players; we just plug and play. While it is highly likely that they would be successful in a variety of situations, you must be thoughtful as these decisions have lasting and far-reaching consequences.

Strategically evaluate what is the most impactful next assignment the organization needs to be filled. That should be balanced with what the employee desires for future career growth. This is one of the trickiest areas to navigate as a leader.

Making an employee take a role that is not aligned to their aspirations is a huge mistake that many companies frequently make. Yes, the employee can deliver in the job but at what cost? You have just told this employee, through your selfish actions, that what he or she wants does not matter to you. Forcing a career move that an employee does not want will absolutely have a negative impact on engagement. A decision like this will damage the trust between you and your employee in ways that may not be easy to rectify.

Whenever there are two career options, you would be better served to present both paths to the employee. This straightforward action will align the decision ownership where it belongs, with the employee. When employees feel they have no control over their careers, they will lay blame on you. The simplest way to avoid this situation is to always put the employee's interest above your own. Even when it hurts.

NO BLOCKERS ALLOWED

As you look at the talent health of your team, watch for blockers in your critical roles. Employees sitting in these positions who have reached their ceiling are considered "blockers." The fact that they will not be progressing upward through the organization results in them blocking the path forward for others. You end up with a bottleneck of talent who are unable to achieve their full potential because there is nowhere for them to go. This is one of the easiest ways to lose your best talent. When employees cannot clearly see a career path for themselves, they question if remaining where they are is a wise decision.

If you have a similar situation in your organization, where a blocker exists, do not wait to take the necessary action. Identify a new role for that employee immediately. Be sure to look for a role that aligns with the employee's current capabilities and aspirations. We should never dump an employee onto another team where the same outcome will occur. Keep in mind, blockers are not poor performers. They are simply unable to exceed their current level.

It will be important that you exercise empathy with the employee throughout this process. You are about to tell someone for one reason or another that they are not properly suited for the role they are in. That is a hard message to hear. You must deliver it with care.

Once you have addressed the blocker challenge within your team, it is crucial that you remain diligent in your talent evaluations to keep this situation from occurring again in the future. There will be times when blockers are inadvertently created. This generally occurs when anticipated future career moves for an employee do not manifest as planned. These situations often develop when one or more of the following occur:

- The employee's capabilities and potential to develop at the next level were overestimated or did not fully mature once in the role.

- The employee's personal situation has changed, limiting their aspirations.

To avoid being blindsided, you need to remain connected to your employees through frequent communication. This will provide you with the opportunity to anticipate fluctuations in career aspirations. As your employees' lives unfold, their preferences of work locations, hours, and experiences will change. Their new goals may deviate from your original plan. You will also be in a better position to rapidly address any unforeseen capability gaps.

DON'T STACK THE DECK

Avoid a stacked deck of ready-now people. If you have multiple employees ready for their next assignment but have no available seats on the horizon, you have some work to do. Keeping those employees challenged must remain one of your top priorities. Providing your employees with alternative learning opportunities is one way of keeping them engaged.

This can include providing them broader scope in their current role or identifying a special assignment that enables them to learn and develop a new skill.

Keep in mind, this is a short-term measure. Highly talented people know they are highly talented. They also know when the organization is not being fair. You expect your employees to work hard and deliver against their objectives. In return, your employees expect that if they work hard and deliver against their objectives they will receive career advancement opportunities. It is a mutually beneficial relationship, but you have to keep up your end of the bargain.

Even with the best-laid succession plan, situational timing does have a dramatic impact on your ability to execute the plan. It is understandable that you would prefer to keep your top talent within your team ranks; however, at times that is not a viable option. On occasion, you may have no choice but to look beyond your desires. Exporting top talent for the good of the organization is a win-win situation. The company will have a stronger future. At the same time, it will increase the chances that your employees will remain engaged and satisfied with their careers.

Those considered high-potential talent understand their worth internally. These employees absolutely know their value externally in the marketplace. You would be naïve to think that these employees will stick around any longer than they have to when the company is not meeting their career needs. If you are unable or unwilling to supply them with the advancement opportunities they have earned, they are going to find a company who will value what they can contribute.

GET OUTSIDE PERSPECTIVE

As you are working through your succession plan, be sure to gather a cross-functional perspective. You need to understand how your employee is viewed throughout the organization. Before finalizing your plan, obtain the necessary feedback regarding the employee's ability to perform the role you have envisioned.

This is especially important when planning succession into leadership positions. Speaking with colleagues across the broader organization, you will want to understand and learn:

Can this employee work well with other teams?

Does he or she have high emotional intelligence?

Can he or she lead up, down, and across the organization?

Getting this early buy-in from co-workers will set your employees up for success as they develop their leadership capabilities. They will have the cross-functional support in their new roles necessary to enable strong collaboration. This feedback will also give you the opportunity to learn of any potential challenges the employee may encounter at the next level. Identifying these challenges early will provide you the opportunity to work with the employee on a development plan to address any concerns prior to him or her stepping into the next assignment.

NO ARTIFICIAL TIMELINES

Proper planning with superior execution of your succession plan will ensure the future health of your team and the organization as a whole. Do not allow yourself to get hung up on arbitrary time-in-role requirements. The explanation for not promoting someone to the next level should never be time. If the employee is delivering exceptional results, who really cares how long they have been in the role? An employee should never be or feel intentionally penalized for being better than average.

TAKE BALANCED RISKS

Do not be afraid to give someone a stretch assignment. As with most things, succession plans are fluid; they are never set in stone. When an opportunity presents itself, be willing to take a risk. Have confidence that you have developed your people well. Trust that they are willing and able to live up to the challenge.

Assess areas in the new assignment where there are known knowledge gaps or areas where struggles are likely to occur. Collaborate with your employees through open and honest conversations in which you actively review any and all capability gaps that exist. Creating a plan for supporting the employee's endeavors includes providing the learning and development necessary to close those specific gaps. Taking balanced risks also means that you must strategically avoid making short-term bad decisions.

Oops – Didn't See That Coming!

You have an unforeseen departure of your East Regional Director of Sales. Your succession plan states you do not have anyone ready now, but you have a District Manager that will be ready in about 18 months.

You now have two choices:

- Promote the District Manager into this stretch assignment

- Hire externally

Your District Manager has expressed interest in the role. He is confident that he will be successful in the role but has acknowledged it would be a steep learning curve. After some thought, you decide it is not worth the risk. That region has a volatile customer base, so you will hire someone externally with more experience who can immediately step in and execute the role with minimal oversight. Eight months later you have hired and onboarded your new Regional Director, but your District Manager just turned in his notice.

Your District Manager hid his frustration well but had done the math. He knew that the average time in the role for a Regional Director is six years. So, he made the decision that he would not sit in the same role for another 4½ years once you felt he was ready.

You find yourself baffled, "Why would he leave? After all, I have a career plan in place for him. The timing just was not right this time, but there will be future opportunities." Well, you were looking too narrowly, not appreciating the severity of the situation or the lasting impact of your decision.

This type of situation happens all too frequently. There are only two excuses for this behavior. Neither is acceptable:

- You are selfishly holding the employee back so that you can keep him where he is for as long as possible.

- You are afraid to endorse that employee because he may fail and that would look bad on you.

Leaders are often very risk-averse when it comes to internal talent. There is a reluctance to hire or transfer from within. When faced with a similar situation, keep in mind you are going to take a risk. Whether you hire for the role or fill it internally, certainty is never guaranteed.

The only difference is that with a current employee you know what you are going to get. You should be keenly aware of the capabilities this employee possesses and the work product he or she routinely delivers. That makes it even more painful when you realize that the talent you have lost is due to your own short-sightedness.

THINK BIGGER

Remember to step back and look at the big picture. You should never make a hiring or promotion decision without thinking through the many long-term implications. Evaluate how the individual members of your team will react, both positive and negative. Above all else, be transparent.

If you feel someone is not ready for a next assignment, share your concerns honestly. You must at the same time counsel your employee on what capability gaps exist and how to address those concerns so that he or she will be ready when the next opportunity presents itself. Work with your employee on a collaborative plan, where you both have a vested interest and ownership in the closing of any development gaps.

Before you jump right into execution mode of holding these critical conversations, you need to reflect on a trend that if left unaddressed will hinder your ability to develop top talent for your organization. In the next chapter, we are going to explain how most companies inadvertently classify their employees to the detriment of their own success and what you need to know so that you can avoid making this catastrophic mistake.

8

MISPERCEPTIONS

Our brains create shortcuts for helping us process the vast amount of information that we receive every moment. This is how stereotypes are created. We have all been stereotyped at some point in our lives. In many cases, it happens so frequently that we don't even notice when it is happening. As much as we would like to say as a people we have evolved, the truth is we still do it. But what are the consequences when a company operates in a similar fashion? What happens to an organizational culture that is built on stereotypes?

When stereotypes intentionally or unintentionally are the norm, a company will struggle on every level. It will not only impact the organization's ability to find, develop, and retain their talent but will have a drastic impact on the very ways in which the work gets executed. When you look at an organization's workforce, there are two major classifications that account for all employees. Consider them work types or groups.

Despite common thought, it is not People Leader and Employee or even as simple as Management and Non-Management, though both are frequently used. The true nature of how companies operate today has created Show ponies and Workhorses. All employees are inadvertently lumped into one of these two categories. This classification drives every experience and interaction. Depending on the classification employees are viewed under, the related employee experiences are drastically different.

THE VALUE OF SHOW PONIES

Show ponies have a unique combination of skills that set them apart from the majority of employees in the organization. They can paint an intriguing picture of the future, which makes them fantastic storytellers. They manage up brilliantly, as their communication style and mannerisms enable them to interact well across the leadership circles. The ability to effortlessly network provides them access and visibility that few have the opportunity to experience.

These employees do not go it alone. They will always seek approval and alignment prior to taking action to ensure their direction and ideas are supported broadly. Show ponies do not challenge the status quo. They will focus their attention only on measured initiatives. Show ponies are masterful delegators of tasks and actions. They intentionally refrain from actively partaking in the executional details of their projects and initiatives. This approach is considered highly strategic by many superiors.

THE VALUE OF WORKHORSES

Every organization has a handful of people that they rely on heavily. The likelihood is that you have one specific person on your team that is your go-to person when times are tough. These are the employees that you have confidence that no matter how challenging the situation they can just get things done. Uninformed managers would generally refer to these employees as "executional."

Workhorses are often the most dedicated, hardworking, and conscientious people within the organization. These employees have the drive to achieve the impossible. They are more engaged than your average employee. Management taps into their capabilities because these employees know how to achieve results. The organization always looks good because of that level of commitment and, at times, sacrifice.

THE CHALLENGE WITH SHOW PONIES

Show ponies rise and fall very quickly in today's workplace. After rapid promotional moves, their careers generally stall out as mid-level managers. Career derailment occurs as the expectations continue to rise in correlation with significant responsibility increases. Most notably, if the show pony inherits a mediocre team. Since show ponies move quickly in their careers, they have not had the time to mature their team leadership skills through developing others. As a result, they are often challenged to get results through others. Once measured on the results of the team versus their perceived potential, they can struggle to meet expectations.

They tend to be the project leaders who operate by committee, where everyone has a vote and all voices are heard. This inclusive nature ensures the agreement is constant. However, if unbalanced, this strength can become a tremendous weakness as it does result in slower decision-making.

Most are not adequately skilled at actually delivering the vision they have so artfully communicated. Show ponies often lack followership outside the leadership ranks. This capability gap will result in conflicts, delays, or even deadline misses. Unfortunately, these employees are not equipped to influence employees outside their own classification, which is where the work is being completed.

If leaders are not careful, they can get caught up in the big picture painted and fail to take notice of the lacking results. As is to be expected, show ponies often ride the wave of advancement by moving from role to role as quickly as possible. It is the responsibility of leaders to ensure that show ponies produce tangible results that add measurable value to the organization during their tenure in every role.

THE CHALLENGE WITH WORKHORSES

Workhorses are driven by loyalty and their desire to have an impact. This unwavering commitment to the organization's success is frequently taken advantage of. The traits that make them a tremendous asset to the business can also limit their career growth potential.

Managers love workhorses as they are the ultimate tool. Playing the role of the organizational savior is absolutely exhausting. It comes with very limited perks. Not only do they work long hours, but often with little notice. It is a common habit to drop bombs on them without regard to the impact it will have because it is a known fact that they will always come through in a pinch.

Workhorses often find a way to deliver the impossible. With increased demands and tight deadlines, this may mean they do not have time or patience to deal with the normal practice of stroking egos. Decisions must be made NOW based on all relevant facts and circumstances. Delaying until everyone is aligned to avoid ruffled feathers will not serve the needs of the organization.

Left with few options, they will do what they must in the best interest of the business. They have an unwavering sense of duty to the company and it is this duty that drives their actions. As a direct result of their misunderstood loyalty, their reputations often suffer based on the unfounded presumption that they are not team players.

These employees will strip away the traditional niceties, like endless meetings, if that is what is needed. While it may be uncomfortable, avoid jumping to the conclusion that it is a bad thing. Workhorses rarely have conflicts with others in their classified station. In fact, they are generally highly respected not only among their team but across functions. This occurs as a result of their natural tendency to collaborate with cohorts to identify a common solution. They can get frustrated; however, it is with the lack of momentum. Delays that are seen as unnecessary will cause them to push forward independently.

Workhorses can feel that they are being taken for granted and unappreciated. This is often an accurate assessment. Many of these employees have been pigeonholed in their current roles while their career aspirations go unfulfilled. Eventually, these employees that are relied so heavily on will come to realize that the company does not appreciate the continued sacrifice they make. Even more disconcerting is the realization that the ability to achieve their professional goals within your company is no longer a practical option. This will cause them to react out of frustration. That reaction results in the employee looking for new opportunities outside of your organization.

Without empathy, you run the risk of pushing too hard for too long. This environment will burn out even your best talent. An unbalanced relationship between the organization and its workhorses will undoubtedly increase turnover and result in a significant loss in critical executional knowledge. These are the types of exits that companies find most painful, as workhorses leave behind a gaping hole that is broadly felt throughout the entire organization.

DON'T PLAY WELL TOGETHER

Workhorses and show ponies do not play well together. There is a lack of understanding or appreciation for what the other brings to the table. This often manifests as poor execution or siloed operations. When left alone to fester, these deep-rooted conflicts can be quite challenging to resolve.

There are two reasons for this lack of collaboration. First, because the issues often go undetected by senior leaders until there is a significant negative impact on the business results. By this point, the problems are embedded; therefore, they are not so easily addressed. Second, senior leaders simply refuse to acknowledge the problem or intentionally choose to ignore the underlying issues.

This conflict exists on a daily basis. Discord affects every interaction that takes place throughout your business. While there are likely situations that arise where the lack of collaboration becomes more prominent, know that it is always there. The dysfunction will undoubtedly remain until the organization changes the way it operates. Therefore, we must stop with the classifications that divide the population.

HOW DID YOU GET HERE?

How did we get to a place where companies and leaders actively engage in classification of employees and why has no one noticed the damaging effects this has on running the business? The truth is when it is the standard and how things are done, most people don't even notice. It likely seemed a bit odd when you first arrived, but at this point you are embedded into the culture. You have assimilated.

Unfortunately, the practice of classification is not done based on fact. When it comes to evaluating employee career potential, perceptions are everything. Once opinions have been formed and employees have been classified into their designated category, leaders have a hard time altering their points of view.

Regardless of the classification given, these inaccurate assumptions can be detrimental to both the business and the employee. For workhorses, this results in the employee being defined as executional. Even though this is a tremendous skill set to have, there is often the assumption that if an employee is executional that they cannot possibly be strategic. Once viewed as a workhorse the employee's career will stall out, making progression opportunities extremely limited. For show ponies, the risk is high that they will be placed into a role that they have not been adequately prepared for simply because they were viewed as strategic. As you see, neither situation is ideal.

Organizational leaders form strong opinions as they compare their employee's personality against the company's preferred standard. Terms like executive presence, image, or style will be used when discussing employee potential as a justification for lack of progression. While the terminology may vary by company, the results will not.

Conversations that are centered around personality will unequivocally restrict the talent development opportunities made available. Thus, resulting in a talent funnel of those who "fit" the company mold. What few will admit is that fit really means conformity. Those who conform and mirror the behaviors of current leaders will receive a distinct advantage over those who do not. What long-term consequences will companies face if they only hire, develop, and promote people who think just like them?

WHAT YOU REALLY NEED?

Think of the best led Fortune 500 companies. What do all the CEOs have in common? They are hybrids. They are strategic and have an innate gift of conveying their vision to others. At the same time, they have the executional mindset to know how to reach the end goal. One of the key differentiators is their ability to attain followership from all their employees, not because they are the CEO but because each is a Leader.

When companies narrowly view employees in these two very generic groups, what happens to the hybrids? Those employees who have the intellect and skills to supply strategic leadership plus the capability of getting into the details to enable executional excellence. These are the employees that today are overlooked and undervalued. Because classification occurs so quickly, it is often hard for these employees to prove they have the requisite skills to operate in both arenas.

More often than not, these employees are defaulted into the workhorse group with very little opportunity to be viewed in a different light. That being said, not all workhorses are created equal. It is your elite workhorses that are your hybrids.

If you want people who can solve the tough problems where everyone else has failed, you cannot restrict them to coloring inside the lines. It is not a realistic expectation. To truly realize the full potential of your hybrid population, you must appreciate that their methods will be unique. Avoid trying to change them or force them to conform to what the current normal is. They are not like everyone else, nor do they need to be in order to add value to the organization.

In time, conformity will be the death of companies. You cannot say that you want to drive change or innovation but then only listen to opinions that match your own. To truly be effective, individuals must not be excluded for having a different point of view or punished based on their personality. If professional success requires conforming to the current culture, how does the business environment ever change or improve?

NOW, WHAT DO I DO?

Now that you are aware of this unconscious classification that frequently occurs, evaluate how you are currently utilizing the members of your team. If you can clearly see the distinction between your show ponies and your workhorses, devise a plan to rectify the situation. You will create a specific plan for each member of your team that is dependent on how the company currently classifies them.

For the show ponies, you need to more closely evaluate their results. You should be looking at particularly what they, themselves, have contributed or accomplished. You may want to assign your show ponies an individual project. This will not only allow them to set up the vision, but also test their capability to execute the details independently. The results will provide you the information necessary to devise a development plan based on results, not perceptions. It is your responsibility to make sure that your employees are ready for the next level. The goal with show ponies is to ensure they are able to succeed at higher levels within the organization.

Your role with workhorses is slightly more difficult. You must identify those employees you are currently using in this capacity. Take time to analyze their performance data very carefully. You should pay specific attention to the time they have been in this role or a similar role, as well as the historical feedback. You are really trying to identify what barriers are keeping them from upward mobility, excluding any data that is tied specifically to personality style.

With this, you will hold targeted career conversations with the goal of understanding the career aspirations of these individuals. At the conclusion of these meetings, you should have a clear view of who your potential hybrids are. It is worth noting that not all workhorses have the desire to progress further in the organization and that is absolutely fine.

This is where aspirations play a large role. To be a hybrid, the employee must be one of your elite workhorses who also wants to progress within the leadership ranks. Now it is time to give your hybrids a chance. Ironically, hybrids' innate character traits - including drive, dedication, and self-awareness - provide them a high likelihood of success. Hybrids do not like to fail. They view every mistake as a learning opportunity. These employees refuse to make the same mistake twice. It is because of these traits that they are highly coachable and engage really well with constructive criticism.

Hard work, dedication, and talent deserve to be rewarded. You must free your hybrids up from the tactical work they are completing today so that they have the time required to show their strategic capabilities. You must actively work to provide visibility to your hybrids from across the organization. This access will change the feelings of leaders over time, unleashing these employees to reach their full career potential.

Keep in mind this is a process. You will not be able to drop your hybrids into a new situation then simply walk away. They will face some significant challenges from senior leaders, especially those with long tenures. These traditionalists want to see results that have previously been unachievable; however, only by using methods they are comfortable with. There can often be harsh reactions to the success that hybrids reach. Frequently, this comes down to change. Hybrids' think-outside-the-box approach to problems is unique and not always appreciated.

If you and your organization have high aspirations for the future, know that without a change to the talent structure it will be a challenge. It is long past time for a recalibration. Your success as a leader is dependent on your ability to develop *all* your employees. This starts with finding the hybrids currently hidden within the organization. Your willingness to support these hybrids and elevate them to achieve their full potential will ensure the company's future success.

9

CAREER CONVERSATIONS

NOT OPTIONAL

Regardless of employee tenure or role, career conversations are a must! Every employee should have the opportunity to share career aspirations and be heard. Employees get very frustrated when they are told that they own their own careers. While it is true that most organizations operate under this framework, it is also true that employees don't know what they do not know.

Your employees want to hear your thoughts and opinions as to their performance and future upward mobility; they have an expectation that should be realized. As their leader, you do not get to check out of the process. You are expected to help each of your employees in achieving their goals.

Career development is an ongoing collaborative process. Interactions are primarily executed between an employee and his or her leader; however, there can be outside contributors like Human Resources and employee mentors actively involved. Each employee's development is based on and driven by substantive career conversations.

When schedules get busy, this is one of the first items that managers will tend to push. Freeing up space on your calendar by cutting out career conversations with your team is short-sighted. Remember engagement is a result of how people feel at any given moment. Consider how your employees will interpret your actions if you consistently cancel, delay, and reschedule career conversations. To put it in perspective: How would you take it if your boss kept putting you off? Like many, you would assume that other activities were more important than you and your career.

Perception is the reality for your employees. Even though it may not be your intention, your employees will feel like you do not really care about them. So, avoid putting these conversations off. This dialogue is hugely important. It plays a crucial role in the relationship you have with the members of your team. Your time is important; this may be the best time investment you will make during the course of your career.

KNOW YOUR STUFF

Leaders who are not prepared give the impression they do not care. Educate yourself as to what growth opportunities are out there for your employees: promotion, expanding the scope of responsibilities, special projects, leading a team, becoming a coach or mentor, etc. Knowing the options is only half the battle. To do this successfully, you must truly know your people.

What are they passionate about?

What type of work do they love the most?

What type of work do they not enjoy?

NOT JUST FOR HIPOS

Career conversations may not be measured, but they are the right thing to do. Everyone wants to feel cared about. Most leaders, if honest with themselves, will say they know that they should be holding career conversations with each of their employees. More often than not, their time is only spent on individuals labeled as "high potential" or those who are being monitored in the company Senior Leader funnel.

These conversations are simply easier to do with high potential employees because of the career trajectory they are on. It is a great feeling, as a leader, to sit down and engage in conversations with your employees about their next career opportunity and know that they can really get there. However, that does not change the fact that every employee deserves to feel fulfilled by the work they are doing. Leaders want employees to aspire for more, to go higher, and to achieve their goals.

One common question I have received throughout the years is, "What should I do if I don't agree with someone's aspirations"? My response is always the same: "It is not for you to crush someone's dreams." You need to be honest with your employee about the challenges that will likely be faced in achieving those goals. At the same time, as their leader, you are responsible for helping them progress on their journey.

During the organizational talent management process, you take the time to designate each of your employees into specific categories. If using a traditional 9-Box framework, in addition to high-potential talent you have those who are classified as properly placed or grow within the role. Notice that the classification is not titled "stagnant in the role." The classification alone demands that you take some action. You should be working to grow the skills and capabilities of those individuals.

When your employees receive the same classification year after year, you are not properly performing the essential duties of a people leader. The ultimate goal should always be to help someone achieve full potential. If you have employees whose capability cannot exceed the average, then you need to work to upskill them or find them a role they are better suited for.

Take a look at the situation from a team perspective. If after evaluating your employees you determine that the entire team is designated as properly placed, you have some significant decisions to make. This means that your team is meeting the expectations and objectives today. Now step back and think about five years from now. If you have this exact same team and they have not developed their capabilities further, how well will your organization operate? Can you achieve future growth with this team? An organization that is not focused on growing its talent will undoubtedly be left behind.

PEOPLE DON'T OUTGROW THE NEED

Avoid the assumption that once an employee reaches a particular level in the organization then they have got it all figured out. I often talk to business leaders about how they are executing career conversations. When most senior leaders and executives are asked if they hold career conversations with their people, they will either say "no" or not as often as they should.

The truth is most people do not know how to have these conversations at all, regardless of level. To be clear, holding career conversations with your team is a necessity no matter who you are or what level you have achieved. Your employees absolutely need your coaching to continue their development.

While senior or more tenured members of your team may not be directly asking you for feedback, it is your responsibility to supply career insight and guidance.

START SIMPLE

Career conversations take practice. They do get easier with time as you learn more about your team. You will begin to understand what motivates them. More specifically, you glean insight into what types of activities or tasks they consider development opportunities. This information will enable you to start with the simple, easy-to-execute actions. As your discussions continue, you will assemble a plan based on the capabilities, opportunities, and goals of each individual that will best meet that specific employee's future aspirations.

Be on the lookout for ways to grow your employees. When you see an interesting article, book, or training, send it to them. This will serve as a gateway to delve into different avenues of conversation, especially if your suggestion is based upon the skill set or career goals of the employee. In other words, do not necessarily send the same material to all members of your team.

You are building EMPLOYEE engagement. Use your suggestions wisely and for optimum results. While you will be holding ongoing development conversations with your team members, you will want to dedicate time to specifically discuss career growth and opportunities.

Just like any other execution plan, you want to keep track of how you are progressing. You must also verify that you are still on track. The same applies to career conversations. Several times per year, you need to check in to see if anything has changed.

What progress has been made since your last discussion?

Are they still interested in pursuing the same path?

What can you do to help?

Career conversations require a time investment. Your goal is to truly understand what your employees are wanting to do in their careers. This should include both short-term and long-term goals. You will need to evaluate what the challenges are that they may experience in achieving those specific goals. With this information, you now have the tools at your disposal to coach, develop, and guide them along the individual journey each will take.

DON'T GET IN YOUR OWN WAY

Career conversations start with dialogue, collaboration, and planning. All of that means nothing if it is not followed by execution. Taking part in these discussions is meaningless unless you deliver on your commitments. It can be easy to get caught up in the day-to-day business operations. If you are not diligent, you will fall short of meeting your obligations.

If you lack follow through in an area that is vitally important to your employees, you will absolutely lose their trust and respect. Your team will question your intentions. Rightly or wrongly, based on your actions or inaction, they will come to the worst possible conclusion: That you are purposefully holding them back for your own personal benefit. These feelings call your integrity into question. This negativity can be avoided if you simply do not get in your own way.

Career Conversations Template

Team Member:	Date:
Likes/Dislikes: 1. In your current/past roles, what specific types of tasks or activities do you really enjoy? 2. What tasks or activities can you do but you don't care to do them every day?	
Aspirations (Professional): 1. How do you define career success? 2. If you could create the ideal job for yourself, what would it be? (long-term) 3. What would be a good next step towards achieving your ideal job? (short-term)	

OUCH – THAT HURT

There once was a young woman who, by all accounts, was hard-working, dedicated, and loyal. She loved her job and the company she worked for. After several years in her current organization, she decided that it was time to see what other opportunities were out there.

She scheduled a meeting with her department head, thinking he would have the best line of sight to any existing opportunities and would be best positioned to provide her guidance as to how to proceed. After spending several days anxiously preparing for this meeting with her boss's boss, she was nervous but excited as she entered the four glass-enclosed walls of the conference room where her future would be discussed.

Employee – "Thank you for taking the time to meet with me today. I wanted to discuss potential career opportunities and get your feedback."

Manager – Clearly annoyed that he had to be bothered with such a trivial meeting, aggressively stood up from the table in front of her angrily barking, "What is with everyone wanting to talk about next career moves? Can't people just be happy they have a seat"? All while never missing a stride towards the door.

You can safely conclude that this extremely short meeting was not productive from the employee's perspective. She exited the meeting bewildered and deflated. From all outward appearances, this once highly regarded top-performer was angry and disappointed. She could sit in her seat doing the same work she had perfected long ago and could do it with her eyes closed. However, it was made crystal clear that advancement here was not on her horizon. That was until the day barely a month later when she approached the Department Head who had been so dismissive of her to inform him that he could have his chair back.

The unacceptable reaction of this Department Head is utterly inexcusable. This executive lacks the foundational skills necessary of all people leaders. The most prominent deficient exhibited is that of emotional intelligence. He is clearly a manager and a poor one at that. He obviously retorted at her with no consideration or empathy of her perspective and feelings. Additionally, he made it abundantly clear that her next career move was of no concern to him.

This is a stark example of how one ineffective manager can have a drastic impact on the organization. If even the top-performers are treated in such a callous manner, what would employees who are simply meeting expectations be expected to endure? Can this organization be trusted to help employees with overcoming their challenges? Absolutely not.

Every action of every leader reflects on the company as a whole. Employee experiences such as this one will leave the company exposed and vulnerable to the dire consequences of significant employee turnover. There are many qualities that are highly valued within the leadership ranks, but being an exporter of talent to grateful external companies is not one of them.

10

DEVELOPMENT PLANNING

EVERYONE HATES IT

Honestly, your employees likely hate this process as much as you do. Why? Because most companies execute development planning as a check-the-box activity; therefore, it becomes an added burden that serves no tangible purpose and provides no intrinsic value. How this is felt and interpreted depends on the type of employee.

For new hires, they are generally very excited to create their development plan. Most appreciate the face time they get with you to gain your perspective and alignment. Only to get six months in and realize that they have had limited time to dedicate to their development plan. Frustration can often follow when they find there is very little support provided that will enable them to focus on their plan.

Employees who have been around a while understand that this exercise is pointless. Once a year, they must spend extra time and energy on creating a development plan that no one really cares about. They are acutely aware nobody will bother to look at it again until the next cycle.

Formal development planning, as it is conducted today, would not be necessary if employees' careers were being effectively managed. Developing strong organizational talent requires leaders to flawlessly execute several critical actions on a frequent basis. After creating a solid succession plan, a leader must hold ongoing meaningful career conversations with their individual team members.

Leaders need to have the freedom, as well as confidence, to take risks that provide employees the opportunity to learn and grow. This includes the opportunity to fail safely. The primary purpose of organizational talent development is growing the skills and capabilities of the workforce to enable company success.

Generally, I would say that employee-related processes are not HR processes. This is not the case with development plans. They are absolutely a product of HR policing non-effective managers. Now, all that being said, you cannot walk into the HR Department saying you are not going to follow the company policy; you are no longer going to create development plans for your team. At least, not yet. So, if you are required to do them, you darn sure better do them right.

You will start by engaging and motivating your employees by using each of the lessons in this chapter. Doing so will allow you the opportunity to develop each employee to his or her fullest potential. Once you have mastered these individual steps, putting them into the required formal development plan is effortless. Think of it as building blocks. You will use the information obtained and trust reached in your career conversations to create a solid succession plan. This forward-thinking insight into your employees' growth, including upward mobility, enables you to quickly assess opportunities as well as risks.

FIND VALUE IN THE PROCESS

If you change the way you view and execute the process, your team will follow your lead. Use it as an opportunity to experiment to get your team access to the new experiences they want and need. Whether you agree with development planning or not, there is something that is certain: Neither you nor your employees are finding value in the process as it is currently structured and implemented.

Today we ask employees to figure out what their current capability gaps are then to identify the necessary steps for sustained improvement in those specific areas. It is comical if you think about it. How the heck do they know? If they knew

143

the answer, it would not be an improvement need because they would have already addressed it.

Providing your guidance will ensure your employees are remaining acutely focused on the most critical gaps. This also encourages their dedication to continued improvement. Gaining this alignment upfront ensures the most efficient use of everyone's time and energy, thereby avoiding the uncomfortable situation where an employee works to develop a skill only to find out that you would have preferred to see them focus their efforts on a different endeavor.

Focus on utilizing the knowledge you have already acquired. Your ongoing career conversations have provided you the information necessary to proficiently help your employees select the correct course of action. Taking the requisite time for consideration will ensure that the path chosen will yield the greatest impact and sustained success. This collaboration reinforces the general commitment that you have for your employees' development.

Additionally, you are continuing to build trust between you and your team. You are earning their trust by actively showing you care through your willingness to aid in their goal achievement. To really get this process rolling and providing some fruitful results, you must encourage your team to move away from traditional approaches. They must embrace a new way of developing their skills and capabilities.

THINK OUTSIDE THE BOX

While training is an important piece of ongoing development, it is not the only element that needs to be considered. Training should be used to build upon the core competencies the employee needs to develop for continued success. Attending a training course is not enough for professional growth to occur.

The training itself is ordinarily a one-time event. It is during this session where participants learn the foundational information about a subject or a particular skill. The true development comes through ongoing practice post-course. Your return on investment will occur with time as the employee deploys and integrates the key course learning into daily actions.

Keep in mind that people learn by doing. You must get more creative when finding or crafting new learning opportunities. To help you start the conversation, step away from the traditional, non-helpful questions such as, "Where do you think you need to focus on for your development this year"?

Use questions such as these to spark your employee's ingenuity when considering areas of focus:

What previous project or activity did you learn the most from? Why?

What is one challenge within our team that you would like to undertake but have limited experience doing?

What task/project would put you out of your comfort zone?

COLLABORATION IS EVERYTHING

Contrary to popular belief, talent development absolutely is a collaborative process. As a leader, you are expected to play an active role throughout the process. Once you have the answers to the foregoing questions, now it is up to you to figure out a way to make those experiences happen. While your employees are focused on doing the work of learning the new skill or competency, you must remain engaged and supportive.

Your ongoing participation will start with you challenging their acquired learnings. This activity will ensure that the intended learning principles were truly understood. Once confirmed, you will then begin to challenge your employee to build on the newly-acquired skills.

Focus on empowering the employee to put into practice the things they have learned. Additionally, you will want to provide frequent feedback to the employee as to how they are implementing and integrating the learning. For the best outcome, you should include areas where the individual has excelled as well as areas where some added practice is needed. When done right, this process can lead to a partnership built on trust and collaboration between leader and employee.

The underlying purpose of development planning is employee growth. Encouraging your employee to experiment by trying something new will ignite excitement if the learning is aligned to areas and topics that she or he is truly passionate about. You, in return, will gain insight into the employee's ability to be adaptable and overcome challenges. You may even figure out what each of your employees is really good at. You have been provided two templates to assist with development planning for your employees.

The Development Planning (Data Collection) Template should be used to gather important information from your employees. This will help determine the areas or topics the employee would be interested in.

Development Planning (Data Collection) Template

Team Member:	Date:
Challenges/Barriers Do you feel like you are currently on track to achieving your career goals? If not, what is holding you back or preventing you from achieving them?	
New Experiences What is something that you have always wanted to try but have not had the opportunity? What is an experience that you think would be really hard but kind of cool? Are there any projects, activities, or committees that you would like to be involved in to help develop your career?	
Expanded Learning Is there another function or role that you would like to learn more about? Would you like to obtain a mentor? If yes, is there someone internally that you feel would be a good mentor for you?	

The Development Planning (Action Plan) Template is used to define the employee's goal and outline the specific actions to be taken for improvement.

Development Planning (Action Plan) Template

Team Member:	Date:
Development Goal: (Define the area of focus. It should be actionable in a short period of time and the results must be measurable.)	
Specific Developmental Activities: (Actions to be taken by the employee to learn the skills and practice implementation.)	
Key Resources: (Who can act as a mentor or coach for the specific action or skill? This person should be strong in the targeted topic area.)	
Desired Outcome: (At the conclusion of the learning, what does the employee need to consistently exhibit to show they have both mastered and incorporated the new skill.)	
Progress Review: (Keep track of the employee's action plan and ongoing progress during your one-on-one meetings.)	
Status: (Record the status of this development plan. Choices may include: ongoing - if the employee is actively working on it, delayed - if you are not seeing the necessary progress, or complete - once the employee has mastered the new skill.)	

Not A Once A Year Thing

Continuous practice in real-life situations is necessary for sustained learning to occur. When your priority is building an exceptional team for the future, you will provide frequent opportunities for your employees to expand their skill sets. Adapting tailored development opportunities to what each employee needs is a unique approach to talent development that will serve you well in the challenges you will soon face. Companies are approaching a time where the environment is constantly changing, where technology evolves with a blink, and teams must be more collaborative with less physical interaction.

Allowing your team to experiment with new learning and experiences that align with their passions will not only help your team adapt to the challenges of the future, but they may very well be at the forefront of bringing those changes to be. For this to occur, you must remain intently focused on employee development. Every situation, project, or challenge should be evaluated as a learning opportunity for someone on your team.

You may be required to complete paperwork once per year based on company policy; however, you should not limit yourself or your team to that time period. If you do, you will stifle the learning possibilities of those you are responsible to help grow. These unique learning opportunities will manifest continuously throughout the year. It is up to you and your employees as to the best approach for taking every advantage of these experiences while they are available.

BECOME A TALENT EXPORTER

As a People Leader, you should take pleasure in developing talent that can be exported to other parts of your business across all levels of your organization. Take pride in this achievement as each employee's career move is a success. It is a great feeling to understand the aspirations of your employees, coach them, and ultimately export them to their dream roles.

You trust your talent to perform to their highest potential. They have confidence in the guidance you have provided and diligently strive to prove you right. Differentiate yourself among your peers by being known as the talent exporter. Once you do, you will see that employees considered top talent will want to join your team for the opportunities that you can and will provide them. Moreover, the organization will continue to look to you to develop their future leaders.

11

PERFORMANCE MANAGEMENT

Performance issues are a painful reality for all people leaders. If you have not already experienced this situation, count yourself lucky but know that it is likely something you will face in the future. Regardless of how good your team is today, at some point a performance issue will develop. You must be prepared to manage any such situation as soon as it surfaces.

It is important for you to be aware of the appropriate actions you can take. This ensures you are equipped to tackle any and all performance issues that may arise. There are even times that performance concerns can be addressed before the situation reaches the severity requiring you to initiate the formal performance improvement process.

The terminology "PIP" may be used in reference to either the Performance Improvement Process or the Performance Improvement Plan. While the acronym may be used interchangeably, it is important to recognize that the plan is executed as part of the overall process. For clarification: PIP, when used in this chapter, is referencing the Performance Improvement Plan.

GET TO ROOT CAUSE

When you start to see a slip in an employee's performance, you must address it quickly. The longer the problem remains the harder it will be to resolve, resulting in a greater impact on the business. There are a few questions that will help you determine the root cause of the performance issue.

Is the employee bored? It may be necessary for you to identify a more challenging opportunity for the employee. When employees have been in the same role for an extended period of time, they can often become disengaged. Roles that are executional in nature or where employees have minimal decision-making ability tend to have a much higher risk of disengagement.

Did you move the employee too soon or was the role too much of a stretch for the employee's current capabilities? It is not unusual to move talented employees into stretch assignments only to see them struggle. We sometimes forget that we need to manage them differently as they adjust and learn in their new role. In this case, you would build a strong development plan with the employee to address the capability gaps that are impacting performance. You will need to dedicate more coaching time to get the employee up to speed and back on track.

There can often be sharp swings in internal opinions of employees. One year they are considered top talent and on everyone's radar. Then they are moved into a new role. Suddenly, we fall out of love with them because they are not delivering as well as they did in their previous role. In this situation, take a moment to self-reflect.

Have you done everything in your power to prepare them for their role? If not, what else could you do to help them be successful? In these situations, you will need to act quickly and deliberately. The longer you wait to act, the more harm will be done to the employee's reputation.

ALIGNING PEOPLE WITH WORK THEY LOVE

People tend to achieve more when they are doing work that they really enjoy. If you followed the advice in Chapter 9, you have already begun holding meaningful career conversations with your team. You know what types of work they enjoy most, as well as the work you should avoid giving them. Now you can use that information to align the work in a way that plays to the strengths and passions of the individuals on your team. This may include an occasional shake-up of responsibilities; thus, allowing employees to swap work in a mutually-beneficial way.

BE ON THE LOOKOUT FOR PERSONAL ISSUES

When you first notice and become concerned about an employee's performance, ensure that there are no personal issues impacting the employee. This generally presents itself as a solid performer suddenly starts missing deadlines or making mistakes that are unusual. Behavior such as this should set off a red flag. If this is the case and you feel there may be something in the employee's personal life impacting his or her work, engage your Human Resources Partner to investigate.

You should never go it alone. Personal matters can be very sensitive. You want to receive coaching before engaging in conversations with the employee. This will allow you to feel comfortable with what you should or should not say. It also allows you to be educated on what assistance is available to the employee.

To be clear, personal issues are not an excuse for poor performance. A leader should never overlook performance issues regardless of the situation. However, it is important that you lead with empathy and understanding. This means looking for opportunities to help the employee where and when you can.

IT'S TIME TO CALL IT

There are times when an employee just is not taking the corrective action needed even after you have done all you can do. Sometimes it is not for lack of effort. It may be that the employee just does not have the capability to do what is required. For the sake of the team and the organization, now it is time to move forward with the formal Performance Improvement Process.

A Performance Improvement Plan (PIP) should never come as a surprise to an employee. If you have done your due diligence, you have had multiple conversations before you get to this point. Along the way, you should be documenting the gaps you are seeing as well as what actions you have taken.

Documentation should include:

- Examples of performance issues (deadlines missed, errors in work, complaints from customers)

- Copies of emails (showing communication between you and the employee regarding expectations set or performance concerns)

- Discussion notes post-meeting (taken immediately after a 1:1 session with the employee where you have discussed the performance concerns)

You will take this information to your Human Resources business partner who will guide you through the internal requirements for creating and executing the PIP.

No Shortcuts Allowed

By the time you reach this point, you are likely frustrated and just want it to be done. I get it. The idea of spending another 30-90 days with weekly conversations and documenting everything seems tortuous, but it is part of a people leader's job.

It is important to understand there are no shortcuts here. The purpose of the Performance Improvement Process is to help your employee get back on track. PIPs are not simply a means to exit an inadequate employee from the company. They should never be used in such a manner.

You Have A Friend in HR

When it comes to PIPs know that HR is your friend, not your enemy. Yes, HR is going to ask you a lot of questions and hold you accountable for following the process, but it is for good reason. Companies generally do not get sued by currently happy employees. Your HR Partner will ensure that the decisions you make as a representative of the company will hold up should you end up in a court of law at some point.

Non-Traditional PIPs

PIPs can be executed for employees who technically meet their performance objectives. These non-traditional PIPs are used when an employee's behaviors are disruptive to the team and/or do not align with the company standards of conduct.

While behaviors are harder to measure, as employees both what we do and how we do it are equally important. These types of PIPs can be a bit intimidating. If you are faced with a similar situation, reach out to your friend in HR to help you with framing up the PIP.

On the following page, you will find an example of a Performance Improvement Plan created based on specific behaviors that can have a profound negative impact on the team and organization. The deficiency column is used to highlight the area or behavior that is of concern. The actions column outlines some of the activities that the employee must demonstrate to meet job expectations.

All PIPs have a time component to them. You will be meeting with your employee weekly or bi-weekly to review progress. It is important to structure the PIP in such a way that allows you to monitor for progress on this short frequency.

For all behavior-based PIPs, it is advisable that you start with self-awareness. Any employee with behavior issues has a deficit in this specific area. Assuming your employee executes the outlined actions, you will be able to gauge early on if the employee is going to really put in the effort necessary to be successful. Additionally, you will have the opportunity to level set your expectations, as well as provide specific feedback as to the areas the employee feels may be gaps. Do not be surprised if, at this point, you and your employee are not on the same page. It is not unusual. This misalignment will be resolved as you progress through this process.

SAMPLE: BEHAVIORS BASED PIP

Deficiency Options	Actions
Self-Awareness	1. Provide a list of 5 areas or topics where you currently have gaps and need additional coaching or development. 2. Following an alignment discussion, you will provide an action plan outlining the 3 priority gaps for closing and the specific actions you will take to close the gap. 3. Execute all items on the action plan by the due date provided on the action plan. 4. Once a gap has been addressed, explain what you have learned and how you will implement your learning.
Accountability	1. Zero complaints from customers and peers within the organization regarding your communication style. 2. Communicate with your supervisor when commitments are in danger of being missed (prior to the deadline being surpassed).
Cross-Functional Collaboration	1. Build healthy 2-way communication with (Person/People) in (Function). Measured by zero complaints to supervisor regarding your behavior. 2. Attend and actively participate in a positive manner at the following meetings:

MAINTAIN HIGH STANDARDS

Another common mistake made while creating a PIP is to adjust the requirements of what is expected of the employee. Do not compromise the standards of the position. PIPs should not be easy.

You need to be confident that the employee can do the job without the oversight of a weekly PIP review. To self-check that your PIP is properly scoped, ask yourself this question: If the employee successfully completes all the actions in the document consistently, would he or she be on par with the rest of the team? If the answer is "yes," then you have a solid PIP. If the answer is "no," then you need to do some more work.

It is important for the employee to know exactly what she or he must do to be successful in the role. Adjusting the standards for the PIP will send the wrong message. It frequently leads to the employee coming off the PIP feeling good, just to go back on a PIP at a later date because they still are not meeting the minimum requirements. Not to mention that is double the work for you.

EDUCATE YOURSELF FIRST

Depending on the size of your team, you may have someone deeper in your organization whose performance has become an issue and a decision to proceed with a PIP has been made. Make sure that the person who is executing the PIP truly understands the employee's role and duties. After all, how do you know if an employee is meeting expectations or not if you do not really understand the work to be performed? The person executing the PIP should also be close enough to the work to be able to judge how someone is doing week to week.

If you decide the executor of the PIP should be someone else within your team, keep in mind that person must:

- Be at least one level above the employee

- Have a complete understanding of the employee's role and expectations

- Be in good performance standing

RIPPLING CONSEQUENCES

Most leaders strive to have a high performing team. It makes their jobs significantly easier. Unfortunately, it does not always work out that way. Performance issues will inevitably drain the life out of your team. This is one scenario where you do not have the luxury of time. The longer these issues go unresolved, the more severe the impact.

In the eyes of your employees, if you are not dealing with the issue you are condoning it. Perceived inaction on your part will result in a disengaged team. After all, why should they give 110% if the person next to them is not going to? Employees who once trusted you will begin to question your words and actions.

When you are pushing the team to deliver superior results yet one of your employees does not meet that expectation, you must hold him or her accountable. Otherwise, your team of once high performers will lose faith in you. This is a slippery slope that is hard to come back from.

12

RETENTION & TURNOVER

YOU OWN IT

It is no secret that an employee's direct supervisor has a drastic impact on work experiences, which directly correlates to the ultimate decision to leave. While there may be other factors impacting the decision, it is what it is. If your employees are leaving, you own it.

Companies generally track turnover because it has such a high adverse impact across the team and organization. In addition to other measurable results, those with direct reports are evaluated based on turnover rates and engagement scores. These two critical data points are used in the evaluation of direct supervisor effectiveness. Low employee engagement scores and high turnover rates are red flags that will garner unwanted attention.

If you have functional or regional responsibilities, the actions of leaders within your organization are an extension of you. Both turnover and engagement results, as well as any lasting effects, are your burden to address. Your responsibility extends to every single employee in your organization. Therefore, when turnover spikes or engagement declines you must take immediate action. These situations can occur as a result of conflict within the team but are generally a direct result of poor leadership.

Your primary concern should be on improving the workplace environment to stop the bleeding. You must do something now. You do not want more people leaving because you lacked the urgency to resolve the situation.

Doing nothing is not an option for a leader in your position. When necessary, you will need to take drastic measures to sure up your organization. This includes evaluating the effectiveness of the team's direct supervisor. Doing nothing is not advisable.

THE RIGHT WAY

Believe it or not, there is a right way and a wrong way to handle retention concerns. As a general principle, you should never begrudge employees for wanting to better themselves or their family's situation. There is a reason they are choosing to leave and that is okay. You should still thank them for their service and wish them well in their latest adventure.

When a leader behaves bitterly towards a departing employee, it has some dramatic negative effects on the rest of the team. You will see and experience:

- Employees less willing to talk openly about their satisfaction in their current role

- Transparency will decrease as employees will be reluctant to reveal their true career aspirations (internally or externally)

- Trust will erode as your negative response suggests that you do not care about employees and their future

TURNOVER IS TURNOVER

As an HR Leader, nothing irritates me more than to hear a manager say, "Well, Joe is leaving, but it is not a regrettable loss." Really! If you have employees on your team that you do not mind leaving, you should take the time to deal with it now. You don't need an "okay" team. You will never change the game with an average team.

Turnover is TURNOVER. When you attempt to justify the situation, you are simply making excuses for your inability to manage the situation appropriately. If an employee can be labeled non-regrettable, it implies that member of your team was not meeting up to performance standards. No employee should ever be allowed to remain within your team if not adding value to the organization.

By using this term, you are admitting that you did not care. At least not enough to do something about it. You should never delay taking the necessary actions to exit poor performers from the organization.

If you are ever unsure if you should top-grade an employee, ask yourself this: If the employee resigned tomorrow, would I consider it a regrettable loss? If the answer is "no," stop wasting time hoping the employee will quit. Get with your HR Partner to determine the appropriate next steps.

RETENTION BONUS – THINK TWICE

When someone informs you of the intention to resign, generally the first reaction is to try to understand what it would take to keep them. Before getting angry or jumping straight to a retention bonus, take a minute to digest what the employee has told you. Specifically, why are they leaving? It generally is not money that causes someone to leave. Throwing money at a non-money related problem is not the best solution.

When determining if offering a bonus for retention is necessary, you must gather two critical pieces of information. You need to have visibility to the specific work the employee is currently engaged in. You will also need to gain a strong understanding as to why the employee is choosing to depart the organization at this time.

To accurately evaluate the impact of this departure you must consider the following:

Is the employee working on something critical?

Would the untimely departure result in a tremendous short-term negative impact on the organization?

Is there another way to cover the work of the exiting employee in a way that will still maintain the operational standards of both your internal and external relationships?

Employees make the decision to seek other employment for a variety of reasons. You will need to understand the true motivation behind the decision to determine the proper next course of action.

If the employee feels underappreciated, a bonus likely is not going to help. In fact, offering a retention bonus may actually offend the employee. This can occur when employees feel stuck in their roles. Consider the frustration. You have an employee that has been ready for a new role for quite some time. Knowledge of the current role and responsibilities has not yet been transferred to an adequately-trained backfill. Consequently, the employee deserving a new opportunity or promotion is intentionally held in the current role for an extended period of time.

You may find yourself personally blamed for this lack of career development. Although there is validity in that opinion, in this situation a bonus may be just what is needed to buy you some time to resolve this conundrum. Keep in mind retention bonuses are not a long-term solution. Bonuses alone very rarely change the outcome. Employees who make the decision to accept a retention bonus generally leave within one year of their retention bonus repayment period ending.

Do not be overly reactionary to resignations. You do not want to make a habit of throwing money away. Giving someone a retention bonus can buy you another year of service. It will not mend the broken relationship or promise that the employee will remain fully engaged.

When retention bonuses are offered, everyone knows. So, restrict your use of them as a tool unless absolutely necessary. As a leader, you really want to avoid having a string of people at your office threatening to leave if they do not get their bonuses as well.

NO SEAT WARMERS

First, know that it is okay to let nice people go because you are raising the bar on expectations. Standards change over time. There are times when employees are unable to adapt. Second, keeping a seat warm because you do not want to go through the process of finding someone new is a cop-out.

Yes, it takes time to identify talent and get them on board. Short-term avoidance of the problem means that you are carrying dead weight within your organization. The impact of that decision is dramatically worse.

The rest of your team knows when everyone is not doing their fair share. The longer the poor-performing employee remains within your team, the deeper the rift will become. Regardless of the reason, it is your responsibility to address the situation in a timely manner.

If you have seat warmers on your team today, you need to identify the immediate next action to be taken to rectify the situation. You must either find them new roles that better align to their skills or take immediate action to exit them from the company. Either way, inaction is no longer acceptable.

VACANCIES ARE OPPORTUNITIES

Every vacancy is an opportunity to upgrade talent and fundamentally propel your team forward. Take time to think through your future vision for the team. What skill sets are needed to achieve those goals? What gaps currently exist in your succession plan? Where do you want to go? What talent do you need surrounding you to get there?

All teams have competency gaps. This vacancy provides you the opportunity to address these concerns while bringing in new ideas and innovation. Defining what the ultimate goal is for this role and making sure it is structured properly will enable your team to grow and evolve. Adding new talent to your organization is the perfect opportunity to venture into uncharted territory naturally, without causing unnecessary distress to your team.

LEVEL LOAD THE WORK

Your first action should be to prioritize the work. Determine what projects or initiatives can be placed on hold until a replacement is found. For the remaining critical items, be strategic in how you execute the task delegation. You have a whole team; use this vacancy as a development opportunity for those on your team who need to expand or grow their skills. Is there a piece of work that, through your career conversations with employees, you think would help grow a desired skill or competency? If yes, great; give it to the employee.

By level loading the work, you are ensuring that everyone on your team takes on a little so that no one person takes on too much. Be careful that you are not continuously dumping additional work onto the same individuals. Remember, your employees are people. They have personal commitments and responsibilities outside of work. Employees need time to rest and reboot. That is hard to do when you feel like the weight of the team's success is on your shoulders. While this is likely not your intention, it is the inevitable result of constant overload. So, avoid it or correct it as soon as you can.

Be mindful of the impact vacancies have on the rest of your team. After all, someone is picking up that work. Each of your employees is giving up something for the team to survive this challenge. As all of them will be doing double duty for what may be an extended period of time, they are forced to make some hard decisions. They must constantly evaluate what actions require their immediate attention against what can be delayed or postponed.

You must remain cognizant that you have defined the performance objectives for your team. Each employee has committed to achieving specific results by the end of the year. Their ability to meet those objectives is hindered when they are asked to pick up additional responsibilities. When you make adjustments to objectives that account for the current business need, you are placing your employees in a no-win situation.

Most employees will do unpleasant work if it is in the best interest of the business. It is when that work hurts them personally that you will face problems or conflicts. They can either focus on their own objectives, as those results directly tie to their performance rating and pay increase potential, or they can help you cover the current vacancy. They cannot, however, adequately do both.

Turnover is stressful for not only you but also for each and every member of your team. Addressing the challenges that the team will face until the role is filled transparently and honestly further builds trust in your leadership. Now that you have their cooperation, do not take advantage of it. Move quickly to backfill the role.

RETENTION THROUGH ADVERSITY

Managing retention is more critical than ever when you have open vacancies. The longer a vacancy goes unfilled the greater the risk of additional turnover. If you are not careful, the remaining members of your team can feel taken advantage of. There will be some employees who do not handle the adversity well. These employees will look to lay blame for the current situation. Given the present circumstance, you are the natural target.

When backfilling a vacancy takes an extended period of time, employees begin to question what they perceive to be a lack of motivation. There can be an assumption that you do not fully understand how this situation is impacting your employees. An inaccurate conclusion can be drawn that you are in no hurry to fix the problem. This is a very slippery slope.

Once employees turn sour, every decision you make or interaction you have will be viewed through a negative lens. Negativity is cancer! This can have catastrophic effects on the team. It often spreads quickly from one employee to another until you do not recognize your team anymore.

It is easy to spot this behavior, but many leaders are reluctant to do anything about it for fear of making the situation worse. Negativity can be difficult to manage when you have open seats to fill. However, you absolutely must do what is necessary to address the problem. Sometimes simply speaking to the employee emphasizing that this behavior is not acceptable and absolutely will not be tolerated is enough to calm things down. It does not resolve the underlying feelings, but at least can help avoid discontent spreading around the water cooler.

There may be times when even after a discussion with the employee the negative behavior continues. The attitude can come across as defiant, like, "What are you going to do, fire me?" The unequivocal answer should be "yes."

Many times, simply moving quickly to backfill a vacancy is enough to keep a team from crumbling under the pressure; however, addressing negativity and behavior issues cannot be ignored. If that means taking corrective action up to and including termination of the employee relationship, so be it. You must remain in control of your team. When you are able to fill roles quickly, you can feel confident in dealing with these issues as the vacancy gaps will be short-term.

FOCUS ON RETENTION TO AVOID TURNOVER

The retention of your team comes through properly managing the employee experience. If you follow the guidance provided throughout this book, you will see that voluntary turnover declines. The ability to retain your employees is dependent upon your capability and desire to keep them engaged.

Make your employees want to stay. Your actions should reaffirm that they are in the best possible position to achieve their career aspirations. Do not wait until they are ready to walk out the door to try to convince them otherwise.

If career advancement is not a regular part of your consideration and discussion, retention will be a problem. When you do your job well, your employees will feel valued and remain highly engaged. This reduces the likelihood that your employees will be out searching the job boards or accepting calls from recruiters.

Happy employees do not even consider leaving. You have to work diligently to keep them satisfied and happy. Your employees are not unlike you; they want to do work they enjoy, to be treated fairly, as well as to have opportunities to learn and advance their careers. As challenging as it can sometimes be, your job is to empower and enable all these things to happen for each person on your team.

There will come a time when you have done everything right and an employee still decides to leave. Often personal situations impact an employee's decision. In this case, there is little you can do. Try to avoid getting discouraged; it happens. When you get frustrated, keep in mind the only thing worse than one vacancy is two.

13

CEOS – EVERYTHING STARTS WITH YOU

YOUR WORDS HAVE IMPACT

As a leader, your reputation will be your greatest asset. If damaged, it will cause certain downfall for the business. Keeping your word is the foundation of your reputation both internally and externally. The strength of this one attribute impacts organizational trust throughout the business.

Yes, you have a title; therefore, people will listen to you. Those beneath you in the organization will execute what you tell them to do. You should not be fooled by what can seem like support. Employees who simply do what they are told without question are often simply there to earn a paycheck. Employees who are driven by compensation alone will always be on the lookout for a perceived better opportunity to come along.

Loyalty, that is what every CEO should want. These are employees who are dedicated to your cause, care about how the company performs, and do their part to ensure success. They make your job significantly easier. That level of loyalty will only come from trust in leadership. Once you have earned the trust of your organization, you will find that change initiatives become easier. There will be less reluctance amongst your employee population when transformative moments arise because they believe that you will do what is right. They trust you will take care of them.

As the organization's north star, you alone have the responsibility to establish the standards by which the rest of the organization must operate. To maintain a high level of trust, it is essential that you hold others accountable for their actions. The words and behaviors of not only yourself but that of every leader in your organization must align.

You must make every effort to live by the words that you say. You have tremendous responsibilities that only a select few will ever experience. With the constant pressure and demand for your attention, it is often easy to forget that your words matter. How those words are interpreted can have a lasting impact.

Your employees should never question their standing on the list of company priorities. They should never feel that they come second to anyone; not lucrative customers and certainly not shareholders. When your employees feel valued, are supported, and have the freedom to excel, they will deliver superior service to your customers. This, in turn, will generate greater dividends to your shareholders.

CHANGING OF THE GUARD

You must shake up the structure of your leadership team every few years. Having the same team in place over 7-10 years is not effective when a transformation is desired. You need an influx of innovative thought. Those who are in roles for an extended period have a much harder time with change. Senior leaders resistant to change will grind your initiatives to a halt if you allow them to.

For many, you inherited the leadership team from your predecessor. You cannot expect to drive change when the old leader's people surround you. You may find reluctance, which masquerades as fake support, stalling every change you try to institute. If you find yourself in a situation where the conversations never end so that the actions can begin, you probably need to shake up the team.

YOUR LEADERSHIP TEAM MATTERS

Surround yourself with vocal leaders. Individuals who are willing to challenge your opinions and suggestions. If you look around and your entire team is trying to impress you, it may boost your ego a bit, but you will inevitably make bad decisions as a result.

At this point, you have meticulously outlined the performance expectations of each of your leaders. You monitor the progress of each on a frequent basis. I would ask that you pause to reflect on how much emphasis you have placed on the people management side of performance. Do your leaders operate against substantial people-related objectives that are tied to their bonus potential? While we would love for people to simply do the right thing, unfortunately, most people do what is measured and rewarded.

People-related metrics vary by organization but include the following:

- Time to fill open positions

- Turnover rates

- Engagement scores

I challenge you to expand your expectations further. Are your leaders strategically developing people for future roles? Are they filling in current capability or leadership gaps within the organization? Including metrics on succession planning helps ensure the viability of your organization. Your objective is to balance enabling your leaders to achieve the short-term organizational goals while also maintaining a line of sight on the capability and competency needs of the future talent.

Take time to consider the role you want your leaders to play when it comes to organization and talent development. Then clearly define and communicate your expectations to your leadership team, as well as the broader employee base. More importantly, hold them accountable to live up to those expectations. If you have managers who deliver strong results as traditionally measured but have built no leadership bench or treat people poorly, you must cut them loose.

You cannot afford toxic behavior at any level, but it is even more damning when they are sitting at your leadership table. The company will not reach its full potential when you are carrying that kind of baggage. You will never earn the support or respect from your organization while these behaviors remain unaddressed. Be mindful, your employees will always blame you for the actions of those beneath you. While it may be unintentional, to others inaction means that you condone the methods and results regardless of the impact.

PRACTICE THOUGHTFUL QUESTIONING

You don't need to know all the answers. Just make sure that you are giving a seat at the table to those individuals in your organization who do. Odds are that is not your leadership team, as they are not the ones in the trenches. Remember you have an entire organization behind you who will support you in making decisions. You don't need to go it alone!

Every behavior you exhibit will be replicated and trickled down through your organization. If you question every decision made or action taken, your senior leaders will do the same but for a very different reason. This is, of course, assuming you are not just trying to exercise control and you have a legitimate reason for needing to investigate. Your leadership team, however, will suffocate their teams, micromanaging every detail, all so that they acquire an answer to a question you may or may not ask. Why? So they look good. They are just trying to impress you. No one, regardless of level, wants to admit to not having all the answers, especially to the boss.

Stop rewarding your leadership team for knowing every detail on all projects because you are inadvertently creating a culture that lacks trust. Frankly, that is not the job you want them to do. They should not be gatekeepers of information. They should be focused on the strategic initiatives and delivering on the future vision you have outlined for your organization.

By allowing them to get into the weeds, you are slowing down the progress you are trying to achieve. Instead of asking a question and expecting an immediate answer, you would be better served to ask, "Who on the team can tell us about the project"? Then, if you really wanted to know, talk to that person directly.

GET TO KNOW YOUR PEOPLE

If you can jump on an assembly line and no one has the slightest clue who you are, you have a significant problem. People do not trust someone that they do not know. You need to dedicate time. Then make it a priority to get out to meet the people in your organization. Simply holding a quarterly all-hands meeting will not suffice. Would you trust someone that you only saw every few months, whose only purpose in showing up was to give you the latest business update? Of course not.

To be clear, I am not talking about a once a month walk around the warehouse. You do not get credit for doing the basics. Those interactions are limited and lack quality. To build trust, you need to know your employees and they need to know you. When you walk down the hallways you should know the names of the people you are passing. Take these opportunities to be present and engage in conversation with those around you. Showing interest in your employees through these simple interactions goes a long way in changing the hearts and minds of the organization.

Challenge yourself to build a robust network internally. Generally, we network with those that we feel we can learn from. Most often those interactions are with individuals at our career level. Have you established a network that spans the depth of your organization? At this point in your career, the people you need to learn from the most are much deeper in the organization than you currently interact with.

YOU NEED TO KNOW THE HARD TRUTHS

Find a brutally honest coach or two. It is preferable that this person not directly report to you. These employees will be your eyes and ears on the ground to help you understand the climate of your organization. They will be able to provide you insight as to how you are perceived across the organization. This person's purpose should be to hold a mirror up to enlighten you as to the things that no one else would dare say. They will also provide you coaching as to how to address any challenges or concerns the general population is experiencing.

Think twice before you proceed down this road. If your ego cannot take someone's honest feedback, do not ask for it. You must have a high level of emotional intelligence to request and receive this type of information. If this is not your strongest skill set, start by closing this development gap before involving others.

For those who want to dig deeper, be prepared to face a challenge. Depending on your organizational culture, this employee may be hard to find. There are few who are bold enough to tell the tough truths, especially to their CEO.

Even CEOs need the opportunity to grow and evolve to ensure that your company remains successful in the future. That can only occur when you have the right people around you. Now is the time to look beyond the board room for that support and learning.

This is a critical step in your personal development; therefore, you must be diligent in your effort to find the right individual. If you look across your organization, there are likely a handful of people who are known for their courage to do what is right even at their own detriment. These employees will always vocalize their opinions without hesitation. They genuinely care about the welfare of others and want to see the company succeed.

If you are unable to find someone with these required characteristics internally, you will need to find an external resource who can provide this service for you. Either way, you must keep in mind this will be a challenge you are not familiar with managing. Having someone tell you the hard truths can be difficult to swallow. If you trust that the feedback you receive is for your own benefit, you will find the exercise will provide you with the knowledge necessary to take the company to new heights.

Don't Undervalue the Role of HR

All CEO's work very closely with their Finance leader and with good reason. I would argue that if your most important relationship is with Finance you are making a huge mistake. Monitoring the company financials and understanding the impact of your operating decisions are critical. If that is the only consideration you take into account, you are completely missing the human element.

To drive change in an organization you need support, cooperation, and guidance. You need a true partner in HR. You can make mistakes and recuperate the losses in most areas of your business, but that is not the case when it involves your people.

You absolutely must choose the right HR Leader to be your collaborative partner. Having the wrong person in that seat can have a devastating impact on your future plans. It is vital that you have someone at your side that you trust, who is aligned with your vision and is dedicated to helping the organization get there.

Your decision as to the type of HR Partner you need should be based on the current and upcoming circumstances. If your business is looking to make substantial changes, you need a proactive change agent standing with you. Do not be fooled by lip service. You must be absolutely positive when making this decision.

While your leaders can subtly undermine your attempt to bring about change, an HR Leader has the ability to create havoc throughout your organization. Remember, the HR Leader dictates all human resources support provided and actions taken throughout the organization. If your HR leader is resistant to change, your initiatives will go nowhere. Unless you are keenly aware and carefully watching, you may become an unwilling participant in a tenure that accomplishes little to nothing. I seriously doubt that was your goal when you agreed to take the job.

YOUR DECISIONS, YOUR RESULTS

As the CEO, everything starts with you. You can minimize the amount of pressure this level of responsibility puts on you by surrounding yourself with superior business leaders who value talent. When you and your leaders operate under a people-first framework, there are few limits to what you can achieve.

CONCLUSION

I have thrown a lot at you, now the hard part begins. Change is rarely easy. Implementing new skills requires that you remain determined even when you face challenges. Your boldness will pay off if you can avoid losing sight of why you are doing it in the first place.

You have likely already thought of a few things that you would like to implement or try. Before you jump right into adjusting your talent processes or scheduling meetings to build better trust and collaboration, I would urge you to do a little self-reflection first. See Leadership Redefined - Leaders Reimagined has provided you important information on how Dynamic Leaders build trust, engage their teams, improve collaboration, and how to execute each talent management process with excellence. You have learned that the business justification for action includes increased productivity, lower turnover, and higher employee engagement. While that is all relevant, those things may or may not truly motivate you. To be successful, you must define for yourself the type of leader you want to be.

Take a few minutes to answer the following questions for yourself:

- Why are you in your role?

- Are you happy and doing what you love to do?

- Are those around you fulfilled and engaged?

- What do you want your legacy to be?

You started the journey of self-discovery and dedicated the time to sharpening your leadership skills. Now is the time for you to practice, evolve, and live up to your full potential. My mission to *improve lives one Leader at a time* starts with you.

Do you want to continue your
leadership development journey?

Attend a
Dynamic Leadership™
course near you!

From people to processes, you will spend two action-packed days learning how to stop managing tasks and deadlines and start leading as a Dynamic Leader.

Targeted development includes:
- Leadership Characteristics
- Leading vs Managing
- Employee Engagement
- Trust | Partnerships
- Talent Management
- Talent Acquisition
- Succession Planning
- Career Conversations
- Development Planning
- Performance Management
- Retention

Visit **fergusonlearning.com** for more information.

Glossary

Black Hole – Time after a candidate is pursued and accepts the employment offer but before the actual start date when the soon-to-be employer dials back engagement efforts making the new hire feel neglected.

Blockers – Employees in critical roles that are unable to exceed their current levels resulting in a bottleneck preventing talent from progressing upward within the organization.

Employee Engagement – The frequent willingness of an employee to exude discretionary effort towards achieving company goals based on their satisfaction with their leader, their co-workers, and the overall company.

Employee-centric environment (framework) – An operating vision centered around the impact every action and initiative will have on your employees that serves as the standard for decision-making and executing priorities throughout the organization.

Employee Experience Journey – The culmination of every essential moment or event an employee feels from the moment he/she first learns of your company to the time of departing the organization that influences the employee's overall engagement.

Employer of Choice – Differentiating the unique attributes of your company to convince candidates engaging with your company is in their best interest.

Followership – The ability to gain trust, support, and collaboration from others to achieve a goal.

HR partner(s) – Human Resources (HR) cohorts who understand your goals and objectives because they invest the time it takes to build a strong relationship with you, who collaborate with the business to drive maximum employee engagement, and who are dedicated and well versed in helping you achieve success.

Hybrld(s) – Employees who have the intellect and skills to provide strategic leadership plus the capability of getting into the details to enable executional excellence.

Internal Customers – Your employees.

Level loading – Prioritizing work and strategically delegating tasks to ensure everyone on your team takes on a little so that no one person takes on too much.

Manager(s) – Members of management who purposefully focus on managing work execution, productivity, and results as the core driver of all actions.

One on one (1:1) meetings – Reoccurring meetings between a leader and his or her employees that provides valuable engagement insights enabling meaningful actions that reinforce an employee-centric environment of caring.

People Leader(s) – Leaders who lead with caring and truly value their employees; they coach and develop their people into strong, highly-engaged workforces who are empowered to take ownership of the daily workflow; who develop a talent bench by providing the opportunity for employees to deliver against their performance objectives; and who then exports top talent within the organization.

Show Ponies – Employees that focus only on measured initiatives where leadership support is high; they are autocratic delegators skilled at networking across leadership circles who do not challenge the status quo.

Voice of Employee (VOE) – Data collected by companies that supplies employee insights and feedback that is then analyzed and used to improve the employee experience.

Workhorses – The go-to employees that management routinely taps into because no matter the situation these dedicated, hardworking and conscientious people know how to achieve results.

Index